What people a

I want to congratulate Father Andrew Miles, OSB for the fine contribution that he has made by his book on the rosary—The Rosary for Intercession and Spiritual Victory. It is a very solid and worthwhile book and I think it will be a great blessing to the people of God and will promote and deepen their devotion towards the rosary of the Blessed Virgin Mary. The meditations in the book should help Catholics deepen their understanding of the rich teachings of our Church.
Most Rev. Michael J. Sheehan
Archbishop of Santa Fe

Fr. Miles' The Rosary for Intercession and Spiritual Victory provides fresh, faithful, and Spirit-filled insights into this ancient form of prayer, so happily regaining popularity. His connection of the mysteries with different petitions of intercession—many relating to common battles of spiritual warfare in our modern times—is inspired. All who love our Lady and her rosary will find their devotion refreshed by this book.
Msgr. Douglas A. Raun
Pastor, St. Thomas Aquinas Parish, Rio Rancho, NM

You came to mind Friday when I was using your rosary book to pray the sorrowful mysteries. How I wish more people could experience your book. It's like my heart is being pulled right up to 'His.'
Thank you so much.
Ann Fisher

This book is an epiphany of how the rosary is a powerful prayer of intercession, a storehouse of blessings, and a powerful spiritual weapon we can use against the enemy. In my opinion this book is an excellent resource that needs to be read by all Catholics. I realize now more fully that by praying the rosary, Mary is using our meditation on the most holy mysteries as a way for us to have a more intimate relationship with her Son.
Eugene R. Valentine MD
Psychiatrist

About the Cover

The cover of this book portrays through images the book's nature and purpose. The rosary draped over the bible tells us that praying the rosary can communicate to us the blessings revealed in God's word. This in turn will fill us with the Light of Christ (the candle and the sunlight) which defeats the powers of darkness. The blue drape represents Mary, the Mother of Jesus, who from heaven offers us her Son, who is the Word of God and the Light of the World. She also offers us the rosary as a way of prayer to receive her Son. The sunlight streaming through the veil reminds us that prayer and the Word of God open the way for the Light of heaven to stream through the thin veil that separates us from the Kingdom of Heaven. Notice also the pattern of vine and flowers on the veil. The earth color of the candleholder reminds us of the humble "earth" of the humanity of Jesus which nevertheless carries and offers us the Light of God. It reminds us that we too are "earthen vessels" formed by the Master Potter and called also to bear the Light of Christ. The white candle represents purity of heart that will enable us to carry this Light and offer it to the world. The "Tree of Life" crucifix on the rosary echoes the Church's cry of faith: "See how the cross of the Lord stands revealed as the Tree of Life" (Liturgy of the Hours, Antiphon 1, Sunday, Office of Readings).

Cover design by Pamela Sneed

THE ROSARY

FOR

INTERCESSION

AND

SPIRITUAL

VICTORY

THE ROSARY
FOR INTERCESSION AND SPIRITUAL VICTORY
Fr. Andrew Miles, OSB

Unless otherwise noted, scripture quotations in this book are taken from The New American Bible, Including the Revised New Testament and the Revised Psalms, Catholic Book Publishing CO., 1992.

Imprimatur: + Michael J. Sheehan, DD
Archbishop of Santa Fe
February 2, 2007

Nihil Obstat: Msgr. Douglas A. Raun
Censor Librorum

Imprimi potest: Abbot Christopher M. Zielinski, OSB
Our Lady of Guadalupe Abbey, Pecos, NM

Dove Publications
Pecos Benedictine Monastery
P.O. Box 1080
Pecos, New Mexico 87552-1080
Phone: (505) 757-6597
Fax: (505) 757-3445
http://www.pecosmonastery.org/dove/dove.html
ISBN 1-931598-17-0   Paperback
ISBN 1-931598-18-7 eBook

Published by Dove Publications, Copyright 2011

My mother, Mary Louise Tobin Miles, praying her rosary

Dedication

I dedicate this book

- to the praise and honor of our Lord Jesus Christ who won for us such a great salvation through his holy mysteries.
- to the honor of the Blessed Virgin Mary, Mother of Jesus, who shared so deeply in the mysteries of her Son.
- to the memory of my mother, Mary Louise Tobin Miles, who prayed so many rosaries for her children and for others.
- to the memory of countless others who have sent their prayers heavenward through the holy rosary and from whose prayers we still benefit today.

ACKNOWLEDGEMENTS

Many people have contributed to the publication of this book. Even at the risk of omitting some, I would like to mention with gratitude some who have been most helpful. A special thanks to those who for years have been encouraging me to write, particularly Sr. Ann Cic, OSB, and Page Zyromski. For editing assistance and other valuable insights, I am especially grateful to Sr. Pat Schubauer, Betsy Serafin, Ann Applegarth, and Linda Rowley Blue. I likewise owe a special thanks to Pamela Sneed for her spiritual insights and her much appreciated computer skills. For valuable comments and suggestions I would also like to thank Virginia Molinari, and my sister-in-law Maria Miles. This book would also not have come into being without the valuable insights I received on spiritual warfare from Mella (pseudonym requested to protect privacy). I am also especially grateful to Jim and Carolyn Moraniec for their prayers and financial assistance. I likewise owe a debt of gratitude to Mary Sneed for the beautiful sketches with which she has so richly embellished this book and to Mike Edris for his invaluable assistance. So many others have also contributed to this book with their suggestions and financial contributions. To all of these I am most grateful.

CONTENTS

PART I

PART II

PART III
Making Our Prayer More Effective............................... 137

ABOUT THE AUTHOR

Fr. Andrew Miles, OSB, is a Benedictine monk of Our Lady of Guadalupe Abbey in Pecos, New Mexico. He made his first vows at Holy Cross Abbey in Canon City, Colorado, on July 11, 1955 and was ordained a priest in Pueblo, Colorado, on April 30, 1960. Fr. Andrew served as the second Abbot of the Pecos Monastery from 1992-1997, retiring for reasons of health. For many years Fr. Andrew gave retreats at the Monastery and was the coordinator for the School for Charismatic Spiritual Directors. He is also the author of numerous articles published by Dove Publications, Pecos, New Mexico. In 1967 Fr. Andrew obtained his Licentiate in Sacred Scripture (SSL) from the Pontifical Biblical Institute in Rome. He later studied at the École Biblique et Archéologique Française in Jerusalem.

FOREWORD

"De Maria numquam satis." Of Mary we can never say enough. This medieval adage fits very well, not only with what has been said about the Blessed Virgin Mary, but also with regard to this recent book written by Father Andrew Miles, OSB Oliv.: <u>The Rosary for Intercession and Spiritual Victory.</u> This little gem of Marian theology is proof of our Lady's continual motherly love and protection for her children. Fr. Andrew, both in his public and private life of prayer, has attended the school of Mary where he received the spirit of the Benedictine Olivetan devotion to Mary, so dear to all of us monks who are members of the Olivetan Congregation. Saint Bernard Tolomei, our founder, established a firm course for all his future monks, teaching by word and example the sweet love of Mary. As the sacred lamp burns continuously before the Blessed Sacrament in our churches throughout the world, so too, must our love for Mary be warming and illuminating the interior of our hearts, all too often darkened by evil's insidious influence. Because of the constant vigilance that must mark our lives, we must educate ourselves in the methods of spiritual warfare, prayer, and intercession, which belong to the Body of Christ.

Mary's beads can be a powerful weapon. Do you seek purity of heart? Do you seek to be victorious in your fight for truth and charity? Are you seeking the pathway to mystical contemplation, the heights of union with God, through a meditative, yet genuinely effective intercessory concern for your sisters and brothers? If so, this book will guide you to discover these and other graces in the mysteries of Jesus, which we pray in the rosary.

In the course of the centuries, Mary has visited her children, teaching them how to pray and intercede for God's people. She simply places in our hands a little string of beads and asks us to pray. Inconsequential?

Shall we not rather say, "The beginning of a revolution"? These "roses," meaning the "Hail Mary's," are the seeds of new life strewn on the ground. These "roses" are the arrows of spiritual warfare that pierce the hardest hearts. These "roses" are the substance of charity, directed to their destination by the hands of Mary, given to her to distribute where she knows there is the greatest need.

In the Acts of the Apostles, we see Mary as a woman and mother of prayer. "All these were constantly devoting themselves to prayer, together with certain women, including Mary the mother of Jesus" (Acts 1:14). Her whole life is a basic teaching about prayer. And as every good mother, she teaches us through her example. From this school of prayer, we have a story of the well-known Trappist author, M. Basil Pennington, OCSO (1931-2006), who has published more than 60 books and has written hundreds of articles. After publishing his first book on contemplative prayer, he sent a copy to his aunt who was "highly successful and gifted." She compliments him, but what a twinkle of supernatural wisdom do I imagine was present in her eye when she replied, "But I'll stick with the rosary!"

Through this simple education, through Mary's simple example, through these simple "roses," let us begin the timeless revolution that will continue today as it has for centuries. May we find ourselves under the banner of Mary! With her simple "solution" we will find the remedy for many an ailment! May Father Andrew be blessed for his little work dedicated to Mary and her timeless assistance. May we all be blessed by putting into practice the ancient wisdom offered here through his thoughts, words and intentions—leading us to our heavenly Mother who cannot fail to lead us to her Son: the Way, the Truth, and the Life.

Abbot Christopher M. Zielinski, OSB Oliv.

Abbot of Our Lady of Guadalupe Abbey, Pecos, New Mexico

INTRODUCTION

A few years ago, I never thought I would be writing a book on the rosary. I found myself drawn rather to learn more about intercessory prayer and how to do it more effectively. At the same time I was frequently being asked to help people get free from demonic oppression and so, by necessity, I began to learn more about spiritual warfare.

At the time it never occurred to me that the rosary might be a very powerful prayer both for intercession and for spiritual warfare. However, little by little the Holy Spirit was turning my attention to the rosary. Occasionally I would pray the rosary, or certain decades of the rosary, in the context of deliverance prayer. I found myself calling upon God to release the power and graces of each mystery for the person I was praying for. I began to see God's victory.

I then began to see how the rosary, by its nature, was designed to draw upon all the spiritual treasures contained in the mysteries of Christ. These mysteries, I began to realize, were storehouses of blessings and spiritual power waiting to be tapped.

Then the thought came to me—"Maybe I can help people as they pray the rosary, to receive these blessings for themselves, their families, their church communities, their cities, their country, and for the world. If the rosary is already a weapon for spiritual victory, maybe it could be an even more effective weapon if people knew all it could do and knew how to use it."

As I sit at my computer, I am thinking, "This computer has so much more in it than I know about. It could do so much more for me if only I knew all the programs and how to use them." The same is true of the mysteries of Christ. Jesus once said to the woman in Samaria, "**If you**

2

knew the gift of God and who it is saying to you, 'Give me a drink,' **you would have asked him and he would have given** you living water" (John 4:10). [Emphasis added] These words of Jesus made me realize that we miss many of God's blessings because we don't know about them, and because we don't know about them we don't ask for them, and because we don't ask for them we don't receive them.

God, of course, can give us "far more than all we ask or imagine" (Eph. 3:20), but God also wants us to ask. "Ask and you will receive...for everyone who asks, receives" (Mt. 7:7-8). Recall also the words of James, "You do not possess because you do not ask" (James 4:2).

To assist in the process of "knowing and asking," I have tried to present in Part I, a basic understanding of how the mysteries of the Rosary are storehouses of God's blessings. I have also tried to show how the rosary is a prayer of intercession and spiritual warfare, and how we can pray it in that way.

In Part II I have identified some of the many spiritual blessings and graces that Jesus has obtained for us through the mysteries of his life, death, and resurrection. I say "some," because God's blessings are far beyond what we can imagine. God has "blessed us in Christ with every spiritual blessing in the heavens" (Eph. 1:3). This book will barely scratch the surface.

And so with each of the 20 mysteries of the rosary I have identified some of the special graces that Jesus obtained for us through that particular mystery. I have then formulated prayer petitions requesting these graces. These are printed in **bold** characters, so that as you pray each decade of the rosary, your eye can easily pick up the prayer intention. You can also announce the intention, if you wish, for group prayer.[1] Some space is also provided for you to write in your own prayer intentions based on

---

1   See the suggestions made in Part I, Chapter 3, for praying the rosary as a family. See also the suggestions given in Part II, pages 39-40.

that mystery. I have done this with the conviction that the Holy Spirit will also reveal to you some of the graces that flow from these mysteries.

Pope John Paul II recommended a similar practice when he said, "the contemplation of the mysteries could better express their full spiritual fruitfulness if an effort were made to conclude each mystery with *a prayer for the fruits specific to that particular mystery.*"[2] Although I have proposed that the prayer intentions be announced at the beginning of each decade of the rosary, a prayer could also be formulated at the end of each decade requesting these graces as Pope John Paul II suggested.

One way of doing this is through a simple prayer of thanksgiving. And so you will notice that I have concluded each mystery of the rosary with a brief prayer of faith and thanksgiving. The prayer is, "We thank you, Father, for giving us the grace we have asked for through this holy mystery." If you wish, you could make this prayer more specific by mentioning once again the grace that you have just prayed for. St. Paul tells us that "by prayer and petition, **with thanksgiving**," we are to make our requests known to God (Phil. 4:6). [Emphasis added] The prayer of thanksgiving is also a prayer of faith because it expresses our conviction that we **have** received what we have just asked for in faith (Mk. 11:24) and what is in accord with God's will (I John 5:14-15).

I have therefore intended this book to be used primarily **while** you are praying the rosary. However, I would recommend that you use this book also for **prayerful reading** (*"lectio divina"*)[3] and for either individual or group **bible studies**. With this in mind, I have listed throughout the book, numerous scripture references. In Part I the scriptures tell us about the riches that are ours in Christ and how to obtain those riches. In Part II they are given to shed light on each particular mystery. Readers are encouraged to study these scriptures either privately or preferably with others in a study group. You could parcel out the scriptures in each

---

2   Pope John Paul II, *Rosarium Virginis Mariae*, 35.
3   See the explanation of *"lectio divina"* on page 40.

section as you see fit for separate Bible studies. They are guaranteed to enrich your praying of the rosary and to deepen your faith.

In Part III I have presented some essential elements of prayer that make our prayer more effective. I have likewise added a chapter on the "Hail Mary." The other prayers of the rosary—the Apostles Creed, the "Our Father," the Doxology (the "Glory be"), and even the Fatima Prayer—are prayers that are more obviously directed to God. The "Hail Mary," on the other hand, focuses more directly on Mary. As such it has its own special character and nature. But it also can present difficulties to those who are not familiar with this kind of prayer—particularly for Christians unfamiliar with Catholic prayer traditions. I therefore thought it important to situate the "Hail Mary" within the context of biblical prayer.

In Appendix I there is a section for you to record answered prayers. Eventually of course you will need more pages for this and you could then start an "Answered Prayer Journal." But these few pages can get you started. The more specific your prayer intention is, the easier it will be to identify God's answer to the prayer. It can be helpful, especially for children, to teach them to pray for very specific intentions. Their faith will then grow as they see God's answer to their prayers.

Appendix II contains the prayers of the rosary for those who are not familiar with them. It also indicates which prayers are prayed with each bead.

I have also included in Appendix III a beautiful poem on the rosary which I recently discovered was written by a distant relative of mine, Fr. Abram Ryan. Fr. Ryan was known as "The Poet Priest of the South" during the American Civil War. Among his rich collection of poems was one entitled "My Beads." I'm sure this poem will bless you.

Besides dedicating this book to our Lord Jesus Christ and to his holy Mother, I have dedicated it to my mother who taught me how to pray the rosary. I grew up on the rosary. For many years we prayed the rosary as a family prayer. Even more often I would see my mother praying her rosary as she sat quietly in prayer. In her later years the rosary was her constant companion. Many of the little notebooks she left behind, bear witness to the many, many rosaries she prayed—especially for her children! On page V you can see the photo of my mother praying her rosary. This picture and others like it are deeply etched in my memory.

And yet, like so many Catholics I have talked with, there was a period of time that I stopped praying the rosary. Even now it is not clear to me why I started to pray it again. Maybe it was my "spiritual genes," something deeply rooted in me and in the spiritual tradition of my family that couldn't stay dormant any longer and had to burst forth again into light. I also later discovered that by God's providence I had been baptized in Holy Rosary Church in Alliance, Nebraska. In any case, it was the grace of God calling me back to a way of prayer whose riches I was yet to discover. The rosary now is a regular part of my prayer. I "don't leave home without it."

Going back even further in my family history, my mother used to tell me about her grandmother whom she would care for when she was bedridden. On one occasion my mother had walked partway to work and then remembered that she had not given her grandmother her rosary. She retraced her steps, gave the rosary to her grandmother, who with great joy responded, "Oh, my best friend!"

It is my prayer for you as you read this book, that the rosary will also become your "best friend."

PART I

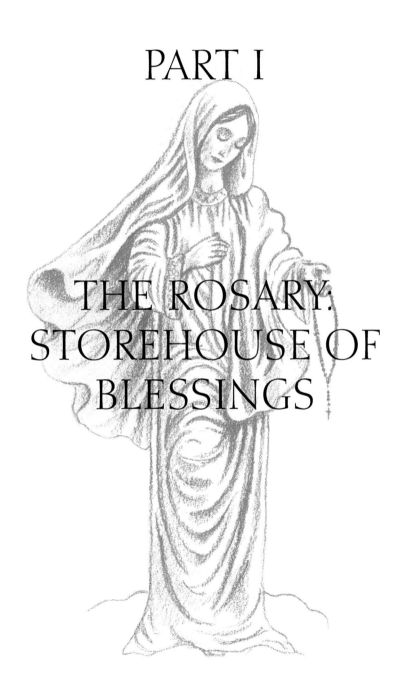

THE ROSARY: STOREHOUSE OF BLESSINGS

CHAPTER 1

WHAT KIND OF PRAYER IS THE ROSARY?

"With all prayer and supplication,
pray at every opportunity in the Spirit."

Ephesians 6:18

Praying the rosary can be a puzzling experience for many, especially for beginners. On the one hand, it is made up of a series of prayers—the Apostles Creed, the "Our Father," the "Hail Mary," the Doxology ("Glory be to the Father..."), and the Fatima Prayer. These prayers are rich in meaning and by their nature invite us to reflect on the meaning of each word and phrase.

On the other hand, the rosary is composed of a series of 20 mysteries (events from the lives of Christ and of Mary) and these mysteries also invite our reflection. And so it seems as if we are being asked to do two things at once—reflect on the words of the prayers (the "Our Father," the "Hail Mary," etc.) and at the same time reflect on the meaning of the mysteries.

Pope John Paul II spoke of how these two elements of the rosary fit together. In his Apostolic Letter on the rosary *"Rosarium Virginis Mariae"* he says, "Against the background of the words *Ave Maria* the principal events of the life of Jesus Christ pass before the eyes of the soul."[4] We might compare this to watching a movie. In the foreground is the action of the movie and its dialogue. In the background is the music, which adds emotion and draws us more into the action. The "Hail Mary's" of the rosary are like the background music. They serve to draw us more deeply into the mysteries we commemorate.

It is fitting that the "Hail Mary's" serve this purpose, since Mary herself was present—sometimes in the foreground, sometimes in the background—in all the mysteries of her Son. She entered more fully into them than any of the other followers of Jesus. Now we ask her to help us by her prayers to enter more deeply into them ourselves.

On yet another level, the rosary moves beyond thought and reflection. It becomes a prayer of the heart—drawing us into loving communion with the "God of the Mysteries," who has sent his Son, Jesus, conceived by the Holy Spirit of the Virgin Mary, and who still comes to meet us in his mysteries. On this level of the heart, the rosary becomes a prayer of contemplation.

It has been my experience that these three forms of prayer—verbal prayer, meditation, and contemplation—all take place during the course of praying the rosary. They seem to intertwine with each other as the Holy Spirit moves through the prayer. Sometimes we find ourselves drawn to the words of one of the prayers. At other times we are drawn into the mystery we are recalling. At other times we simply find ourselves in the loving presence of God. It is best simply to let the prayer happen as the Spirit leads.

---

4   Pope John Paul II, Apostolic Letter *Rosarium Virginis Mariae*, 2.

Where then does this book fit in? Is the rosary also a prayer of intercession and spiritual warfare? Doesn't this just complicate the matter? Actually intercession and spiritual warfare flow naturally out of the prayers and the mysteries of the rosary. The whole purpose of God is to draw us—and the whole world—into the saving work that he has accomplished for us through the mysteries of his Son.

Intercession brings all the graces and blessings of each mystery into our lives and the lives of those for whom we pray. God's work of salvation is complete in what Jesus did for us. But on our part we must appropriate it—make it our own. This we do through intercession and spiritual warfare. Through the rosary (as well as through other prayers) we join our prayers with the prayers of Jesus, who always lives to make intercession for us. (See Hebrews 7:25.) We also join with Mary and with the saints and angels who, together with Jesus, make intercession before the throne of God.[5]

---

5   For descriptions of this heavenly intercession see Revelation 6:9-10 and 8:3-4. See also II Maccabees 15:14.

CHAPTER 2

THE MYSTERIES: STOREHOUSES OF SPIRITUAL TREASURES

*"For in him dwells the whole fullness of the deity bodily
and you share in this fullness in him."*

Colossians 2:9-10

Jesus is the storehouse of spiritual treasures. In fact, Paul says, God "has blessed us in Christ with **every** spiritual blessing in the heavens" (Eph. 1:3). [Emphasis added]

God has decided to give us EVERYTHING that he possesses! In order to do this, he has deposited all of his treasures in his Son, so that by receiving Jesus we will also receive every one of his blessings. If God "did not spare his own Son," Paul says, "but handed him over for us all, how will he not also give us everything else along with him?" (Rom. 8:32). Pope John Paul II also said that all Christ's riches "are for every individual and are everybody's property."[6]

---

6   See *Catechism of the Catholic Church*, 519.

Nothing gives God greater pleasure than to give gifts to his children. The more God gives us, the happier he is. We call this God's **glory**. "By this is my Father glorified, that you bear much fruit and become my disciples" (John 15:8). The more we receive God's gifts and blessings, the more God is glorified—and the happier we become as well.

How then do we receive God's blessings? Let us now explore the answer to this question.

The Mysteries of Jesus

Jesus began to merit for us the blessings and promises of God from the first moment of his conception. He continued to merit them at each moment of his life by everything he did for our salvation. By living his human life perfectly in love and in obedience to the Father's will, Jesus obtained for us every grace and spiritual blessing. All the events of Jesus' life, therefore—which we call his mysteries—have become for us the sources or storehouses of God's blessings.

We can never know, of course, in this life, all that Jesus did for us. St. John tells us that if we tried to write down everything Jesus did, not even the whole world could contain the books that would have to be written. (See John 21:25.) That is why the authors of the New Testament chose to write down for us those events in the life of Jesus that they considered to be of "first importance" (I Cor. 15:3). We read of these now in the Scriptures.

The Mysteries of the Rosary

The Church has further selected twenty events or mysteries from the life of Jesus for us to recall in the rosary. She does this, not to ignore other things that Jesus did or said, but to highlight those mysteries, which because of their importance, in some way include all the others. For example, the third Luminous Mystery of the rosary recalls "The

Proclamation of the Kingdom of God." This mystery serves as a kind of "umbrella" for all that Jesus did during his public ministry. Jesus proclaimed the Kingdom of God by everything that he taught, by his miracles, by healing the sick, raising the dead, and forgiving people's sins. And so when we pray this mystery, we recall all that Jesus did for us during his public ministry. We could then, as we pray this decade of the rosary, reflect on any one of the many events or teachings of Jesus' public ministry, such as the raising of Lazarus from the dead or the Beatitudes.[7]

Other mysteries that serve as "umbrellas" are, for example, the Birth of Jesus, which invites us to reflect not only on the moment of Jesus birth, but also on all of his infancy. The Presentation of Jesus in the Temple can also serve to recall all the events of Jesus' childhood and how his childhood now serves to sanctify and heal our childhood. The Finding of Jesus in the Temple likewise recalls the years of Jesus' adolescence and young adulthood. All that Jesus did during those years of his life, now serves to redeem and sanctify the years of our own adolescence and early adulthood.

The mysteries of Jesus' passion, death and resurrection are, of course, the great "umbrella mysteries," which in some way sum up and include all that Jesus did for our salvation.

From this we can see that the mysteries of the rosary, far from being exclusive, actually include everything that Jesus did for us, from the first moment of his conception until the completion of his work for us in heaven.

Sharing in the Life of Jesus

As we look at the mysteries of the life of Jesus, we can begin to see our own lives reflected there. We then begin to see God's plan to draw

---

7   See Pope John Paul II's reference to the Beatitudes in the context of the Luminous Mysteries in his Apostolic Letter *Rosarium Virginis Mariae*, 40.

our lives into the life of Jesus so that we can share in the riches of his Son. He has "blessed us **in him** with every spiritual blessing in the heavens"(Eph. 1:3) [Emphasis added].

St. John Eudes teaches this so clearly when he says,

> We must strive to follow and fulfill in ourselves the various stages of Christ's plan as well as his mysteries, and frequently beg him to bring them to completion in us and in the whole Church. For the mysteries of Jesus are not yet completely perfected and fulfilled. They are complete, indeed, in the person of Jesus, but not in us, who are his members, nor in the Church, which is his mystical body. The Son of God wills to give us a share in his mysteries and somehow to extend them to us. He wills to continue them in us and in his universal Church. This is brought about first through the graces he has resolved to impart to us and then through the works he wishes to accomplish in us through these mysteries. This is his plan for fulfilling his mysteries in us.

St. John Eudes then goes on to relate this teaching to some of the mysteries we have traditionally called joyful, sorrowful, and glorious.

> This is the plan by which the Son of God completes and fulfills in us all the various stages and mysteries. He desires to perfect the mystery of his incarnation and birth by forming himself in us and being reborn in our souls through the blessed sacraments of baptism and the Eucharist. He fulfills his hidden life in us, hidden with him in God.

> He intends to perfect the mysteries of his passion, death, and resurrection, by causing us to suffer, die, and rise

again with him and in him. Finally, he wishes to fulfill in us the state of his glorious and immortal life, when he will cause us to live a glorious, eternal life with him and in him in heaven.[8]

Recall also the summary of this teaching in the fourth preface of the Sundays of Ordinary Time.

By his birth we are reborn.
In his suffering we are freed from sin.
By his rising from the dead we rise to everlasting life.
In his return to you in glory we enter into your heavenly kingdom.

This is the wonderful work of God's grace that the rosary is designed to accomplish in us.

Visiting God's Storehouses

The mysteries of the life of Jesus are like storehouses where all God's treasures are contained. But we are often unaware of what is inside those storehouses. As we look at these storehouses from the outside, we notice that they have names written on them: "The Annunciation," "The Baptism," "The Crucifixion," "The Resurrection,"... But most often we have very little idea of what is in them.

What we need to do is to find someone to give us a tour of these warehouses, someone who possesses a complete inventory of them. And who else can do this but Jesus and the Holy Spirit? And so we might imagine that as we pray the rosary, Jesus takes us on a tour to visit all twenty of these storehouses. In each storehouse Jesus explains to us all that he did for us in that mystery and he shows us all the gifts and treasures that are now ours because of each mystery.

---

8   From a treatise *On the Kingdom of Jesus* by Saint John Eudes, priest (Pars 3,4: Opera omnia 1,310-312). See the *Liturgy of the Hours*, Office of Readings, Second Reading, Friday of the 33rd Week in Ordinary Time. See also the teaching in the *Catechism of the Catholic Church*, nos. 519-521.

We have all had the experience of visiting shops and stores and seeing things that we would really like to have. But then we look at the price tag, and we often have to say, "I really like it, but I can't afford it."

And so, as Jesus takes us on a tour of God's warehouses and shows us all the wonderful gifts they contain, it is normal for us to ask him, "Jesus, how much does this cost?" And to our surprise, Jesus responds, "For you, it's free. I have already paid the price for everything here. Everything in the store belongs to me and I give these gifts freely to those who ask me and whose hearts are ready to receive them." "Until now you have not asked anything in my name; ask and you will receive, so that your joy may be complete" (John 16:24).

Mary Full of Grace

We might also imagine that Mary accompanies us on our tour of God's storehouses, in order to share with us her experiences and her understanding of each mystery. After all, she was with Jesus—at least in spirit—in all his mysteries and she "kept all these things, reflecting on them in her heart" (Luke 2:19). (See also Luke 2:51.) She has a deep understanding of them and can help us understand them as well.

Pope John Paul II stated this beautifully when he said, "*Mary constantly sets before the faithful the 'mysteries' of her Son,* with the desire that the contemplation of those mysteries will release all their saving power. In the recitation of the Rosary, the Christian community enters into contact with the memories and the contemplative gaze of Mary."[9]

Not only can Mary help us understand the mysteries of her Son, but she can also help us receive them because she herself received them so fully. When the Church greets Mary as "Full of Grace" (as did the Angel Gabriel), she recognizes that Mary is the one who received fully of all

---

9   Apostolic Letter *Rosarium Virginis Mariae* of the Supreme Pontiff John Paul II, 11.

that her Son did for her. In doing so, she helps us receive these mysteries just as she did, so that we too can be "full of grace"—or as Paul says, "filled with all the fullness of God" (Eph. 3:19). If Paul prays that all Christians will be "filled with all the fullness of God," how much more does Mary pray this for us and desire it for us with all her heart.

How fitting it is then, that as we visit each mystery of the life of Jesus, we call upon her who is "Full of Grace," to help us become full of grace as she was. As so, with each mystery we ask her intercession—"Hail, Mary, full of grace…pray for us sinners." Yes, pray for us to be full of the blessings of Jesus, so that the Father will be glorified in our bearing much fruit and becoming disciples of your Son.

CHAPTER 3

THE ROSARY AND INTERCESSION

"If you knew the gift of God
and who is saying to you, 'Give me a drink,'
you would have asked him
and he would have given you living water."

John 4:10

Once we realize the wonderful gifts God has given us through the mysteries of Jesus, we will want to receive them not only for ourselves but for others as well.

Praying the Rosary for Others

Often we hear people say, "I'm going to pray a rosary for you," or "Let's pray our rosary today for Jim who's going through a hard time." We recognize that the rosary is a prayer of intercession that can obtain graces for others. However, we may not always be aware that besides praying for others in a general way, we can pray for specific graces that flow from each particular mystery.

As you use this book to pray for others, you may want to ask the Holy Spirit to guide you as to which particular graces to pray for.

The prayer intentions that are listed with each mystery may help you pray for these specific blessings and graces. Or the Holy Spirit may lead you to pray for other intentions. For some of the intentions listed in this book there is a blank space that is underlined (_____). You may wish to insert there the name or names of those for whom you are praying. But you may also insert these names with any or all of the intentions listed.

Praying the Rosary as a Family

Pope John Paul II beautifully expresses the value of the family rosary when he says, "The family that recites the Rosary together reproduces something of the atmosphere of the household of Nazareth: its members place Jesus at the centre, they share his joys and sorrows, they place their needs and their plans in his hands, they draw from him the hope and the strength to go on."[10]

When this book is used for praying a **family rosary**,[11] different members of the family could choose the prayer intention for each particular decade. These intentions could be taken either from those given in this book or as each family member might choose (even if the intention does not have an obvious connection with the mystery).[12] Having the whole family pray for the same intention is a special opportunity to claim the promise of Jesus, "Amen, I say to you, if two of you agree on earth about anything for which they are to pray, it shall be granted to them by my heavenly Father" (Mt. 18:19). As you write the prayer intentions in the Answered Prayer Journal (see Appendix I) and later write the answer to those prayers, the whole family will be able to see how God is answering their prayers. This will help build faith in the family and create a greater interest in praying the rosary.

---

10   Pope John Paul II, *Rosarium Virginis Mariae*, 41.

11   What is said here about praying the rosary as a family could also apply to other small groups.

12   It is important that each member of the family be free to pray for the intention that is on each one's heart. This is especially important for children.

We Do Not Pray Alone

Once, a number of us were praying the rosary for a woman who needed deliverance. It seemed at the time that she was not fully conscious and perhaps not even aware of our presence. After we finished the rosary, however, she shared her experience with us. She said that, as we prayed, she could hear another voice praying and she knew it was a heavenly voice. It seemed like the voice of a woman. And the woman was praying the very same prayers that we were saying, except in a heavenly voice and language. It sounded, she said, like something between singing and reciting. It was beautiful. And she said she knew in her spirit that the heavenly prayer that paralleled our earthly prayer was being heard and that it was definitely effective. It was having results!

This experience reminded me not to doubt the effectiveness of our prayers—even when we are not aware of their results. Heaven prays with us. Jesus, Mary, and the angels and saints pray with us in the Holy Spirit. And our prayer in the Holy Spirit is like the Word of God, of which God says, "it shall not return to me void, but shall do my will, achieving the end for which I sent it" (Is. 55:11).

So, too is the prayer of the rosary. It will not return to us empty. Joined with the power of God, it will accomplish the end for which we send it.

The Witness of Sr. Lucia of Fatima

Sister Lucia, the visionary of Fatima, spoke eloquently of the power of the rosary. In an interview with Fr. Fuentes on December 26, 1957, she said:

> Look, Father, the Most Holy Virgin in these last times in which we live has given new efficacy in the recitation of the Holy Rosary. She has given this efficacy to such an extent that there is no problem, no matter how difficult it is, whether temporal or above all spiritual—in

the personal life of each one of us, of our families, of the families in the world, or of the religious communities or even of the life of peoples and nations—that cannot be solved by the rosary.

CHAPTER 4

VICTORY THROUGH SPIRITUAL WARFARE

"Blessed be the Lord, my rock,
who trains my hands for battle,
my fingers for war."

Psalm 144:1

Some years ago many Christians had not even heard of spiritual warfare. Now books are proliferating on the topic. We are becoming aware that, whether we like it or not, we are engaged in a battle against the forces of darkness. "Our struggle," Paul says, "is not with flesh and blood but with the principalities, with the powers, with the world rulers of this present darkness, with the evil spirits in the heavens" (Eph. 6:12). And he goes on to tell us that prayer is one of our essential weapons. "With all prayer and supplication, pray at every opportunity in the Spirit" (Eph. 6:18).

The book of Revelation tells us more about the origin and nature of this battle.

> Then war broke out in heaven; Michael and his angels
> battled against the dragon. The dragon and its angels
> fought back, but they did not prevail and there was no

longer any place for them in heaven. The huge dragon, the ancient serpent, who is called the Devil and Satan, who deceived the whole world, was thrown down to earth, and its angels were thrown down with it.

Rev. 12:7-9

The battle now has shifted to earth. Satan's primary target is "the woman" and her son. "When the dragon saw that it had been thrown down to the earth, it pursued the woman who had given birth to the male child" (Rev. 12:13). According to many commentators the woman symbolizes God's people of both the Old and the New Testament.[13] But she also symbolizes, in a very special way, Mary, the Mother of Jesus, who "gave birth to a son, a male child, destined to rule all the nations with an iron rod" (Rev. 12:5). (See also Psalm 2:9.) "The dragon," John says, "became angry with the woman and went off to wage war against the rest of her offspring, those who keep God's commandments and bear witness to Jesus" (Rev. 12:18).

Once when I was engaged in a conversation with an ex-Satanist who had only recently become a Christian, she suddenly handed me a list she had made of the ten things that Satan hates most. To my surprise, at the very head of the list—in first place—was "Mary and the Rosary." She told me, "Satan hates Mary." Why would this be? Perhaps it is because he knows that Mary—through her Son and together with the rest of her offspring—will bring about his defeat.

I was also surprised that she put the rosary at the head of the list. She had only been a Catholic a short time and was not familiar with Catholic devotions. Was she picking up in the Spirit that Satan hated the rosary so much because he knew it would be the weapon of his defeat?

---

13   See the footnote in the *New American Bible* on Revelation 12:1-6: "The woman adorned with the sun, the moon, and the stars (images taken from Gn 37,9-10) symbolizes God's people in the Old and the New Testament."

The Rosary a Weapon of Spiritual Warfare

After my conversation with the ex-Satanist I also came across the following account of Fr. Gobbi regarding the rosary as a weapon of spiritual warfare. He relates how Mary gave him an understanding of the meaning of the vision in Revelation 20:1-3 about how Satan will be chained and thrown into hell—which is then locked and sealed so that he can no longer lead the nations astray.

> The chain, with which the great Dragon is to be bound, is made up of prayer made with me and by means of me. This prayer is that of the holy rosary. A chain has in fact the function of first of all limiting action, then of imprisoning, and finally of making ineffective every activity of the one who has been bound by it.

> The chain of the holy rosary has first of all the function of limiting the action of my Adversary. Every rosary which you recite with me has the effect of restricting the action of the Evil One, of drawing souls away from his pernicious influence, and of giving greater impetus to the expansion of goodness in the life of many of my children.

> The chain of the holy rosary has also the effect of imprisoning Satan, that is, of making his action impotent, and of diminishing and weakening more and more the force of his diabolical power. And so, each rosary which is recited well deals a mighty blow to the power of evil, and it represents one part of his reign which is destroyed.

> The chain of the holy rosary brings about, in the end, the result of making Satan completely harmless. His great power is destroyed. All the evil spirits are cast into the

pool of fire and sulfur; the door is shut by me with the key of the power of Christ, and thus they will no longer be able to go out into the world to do harm to souls.[14]

The Mysteries of Jesus and Spiritual Warfare

How is the rosary a weapon for spiritual victory? We can understand this, when we realize that the rosary draws upon the power and the graces that are present in all of the mysteries of Jesus.

St. John says that "the Son of God was revealed to destroy the works of the devil" (I John 3:8). Jesus destroys the works of the devil by doing the **works of God**. The works of God undo and destroy the works of the devil. Whatever works of evil and deception that Satan has worked and will work in the human race from Adam and Eve until the end of time, Jesus has destroyed by re-doing all of our works in God.

Satan begins his work in us from the first moment of our conception. "I was born guilty," the Psalmist says, "a sinner, even as my mother conceived me" (Ps. 51:7).[15] We inherit a fallen, sinful nature infected with spiritual blindness and a tendency toward rebellion and disobedience. Jesus re-does, re-makes, our conception through his own conception, which was totally free from any influence of sin and Satan. Through the mystery of Jesus' conception (the first Joyful Mystery) our own conception is healed, so that from the very first moment of our lives, our whole being can be directed toward God.

By his entire life which was lived in God and for God, Jesus reversed the effects of sin in our lives, from the first moment of our conception until

---

14   See in the writings of Fr. Gobbi for the *Marian Movement of Priests* the entry for October 7, 1992, no. 479.

15   See the explanation of this reality in the *Catechism of the Catholic Church*, nos. 388-421.

our death. Our whole life is healed and set free from the effects of the devil by the life, death, and resurrection of Jesus.

Therefore, as we pray the mysteries of Jesus from his conception to his ascension into heaven, our own lives are re-made in the life of Jesus. His life becomes our life. Our lives are healed and restored, and the works of the devil are destroyed in us. And, by praying the rosary as intercession and spiritual warfare, we can obtain these same graces for those for whom we pray.

Spiritual Warfare and Particular Mysteries

Jesus' work of destroying the works of the devil can be seen especially in certain mysteries where Jesus very clearly engages in spiritual warfare. Even though some of this will be evident in the petitions given for these mysteries in Part II, it is helpful to highlight some of them here.

The following are a few examples taken from the various groups of mysteries.

From the Joyful Mysteries

Through the mystery of his Incarnation (first Joyful Mystery), Jesus destroys the original work of the devil by healing the effects of original sin in us, particularly our spiritual blindness (see II Corinthians 4:4) and our inclination to sin (see Romans 7:14-25). And so, as we pray this mystery, we can receive this healing for ourselves and for others.

From the Luminous Mysteries

At his Baptism in the Jordan (first Luminous Mystery), Jesus was revealed as the "Lamb of God" who took upon himself all the sins of the world. God made him "to be sin who did not know sin, so that we might become the righteousness of God in him" (II Cor. 5:21). Jesus is also empowered by the Holy Spirit at his baptism to fight against Satan, and he immediately overcomes all of Satan's temptations during his forty days in the desert. And so in this mystery we can receive from Jesus the cleansing of our sins, the righteousness of God, and victory over the devil's temptations.

In his Proclamation of the Kingdom of God (third Luminous Mystery), Jesus went about "driving out demons throughout the whole of Galilee" (Mk. 1:39) and healing all those oppressed by the devil" (Acts 10:38). He wants to do the same for his people now.

From the Sorrowful Mysteries

It is especially in the sorrowful mysteries that we see Jesus doing battle against Satan and destroying Satan's power.

In his Agony in the Garden (first Sorrowful Mystery), Jesus rejects Satan's temptations to turn aside from his sufferings and death. Jesus chooses to do the will of his Father rather than follow his own human will. Jesus now obtains this same grace for us.

Through his Death on the Cross (fifth Sorrowful Mystery), Jesus destroys sin and death and all the power of Satan. "He himself bore our sins in his body upon the cross, so that, free from sin, we might live for righteousness. By his wounds you have been healed" (I Pt. 2:24). By atoning for our sins, Jesus removed Satan's claim against us, "nailing it to the cross; despoiling the principalities and the powers, he made a public spectacle of them, leading them away in triumph by it" (Col. 2:14-15). Through Jesus' death on the cross, God has "delivered us from the power of darkness and transferred us to the kingdom of his beloved Son" (Col. 1:13). When you pray this mystery of the rosary, you are praying victory!

From the Glorious Mysteries

Jesus' Resurrection (first Glorious Mystery) reveals God's victory over sin, death, and all the powers of hell. Jesus is the beginning of God's new creation, which is now reconciled to God. In him we too are raised from death to life and inherit God's eternal Kingdom. As we pray this mystery of the rosary, we share in Jesus' resurrection and reclaim our heavnly inheritance as sons and daughters of God. "Death no longer has power over him," Paul says (Rom. 6:9), and when we live in him, it no longer has power over us. Our victorious King has conquered!

Jesus Ascends to Heaven (second Glorious Mystery) and is enthroned at the right hand of the Father as King and Lord of all. God has, in the words of the psalm, "put all things under his feet" (Ps. 8:7; I Cor. 15:27; Eph. 1:22; Heb. 2:8). Jesus says, "All power in heaven and on earth has been given to me" (Mt. 28:18). As we pray this mystery, Jesus' power becomes our power to overcome the forces of evil. (See Luke 10:19; Romans 8:37-39.)

"You will receive power, Jesus said, "when the holy Spirit comes upon you" (Acts 1:8) (third Glorious Mystery). The powers of hell are no match for the power of the Holy Spirit. As we pray this mystery of the rosary, we call upon the power of the Holy Spirit for ourselves and for others.

Truly, as we finger the beads of the rosary, it is God who trains our hands for battle, our fingers for war (Ps. 144:1). And we say with St. Paul, "thanks be to God who gives us the victory through our Lord Jesus Christ" (I Cor. 15:57).

32

PART II

THE MYSTERIES
AND
THEIR GIFTS

CHAPTER 5

THE TWENTY MYSTERIES OF THE ROSARY

PART II of this book is designed to help you to know, understand, and make your own the rich graces and blessings Jesus has obtained for us in each of the twenty mysteries of the rosary: the five Joyful Mysteries, the five Luminous Mysteries, the five Sorrowful Mysteries, and the five Glorious Mysteries.

The following are the twenty mysteries:

The Five Joyful Mysteries
(Traditionally Prayed on Mondays and Saturdays)
1. The Annunciation to Mary of the Incarnation
2. The Visitation of Mary to Elizabeth
3. The Birth of Jesus
4. The Presentation of the Child Jesus in the Temple
5. The Finding of Jesus in the Temple

The Five Luminous Mysteries
   (Traditionally Prayed on Thursdays)
1. The Baptism of Jesus in the Jordan
2. The Wedding Feast at Cana
3. The Proclamation of the Kingdom of God
4. The Transfiguration of Jesus
5. The Institution of the Holy Eucharist

The Five Sorrowful Mysteries
   (Traditionally Prayed on Tuesdays and Fridays)
1. The Agony Of Jesus in the Garden
2. The Scourging of Jesus at the Pillar
3. The Crowning of Jesus with Thorns
4. Jesus Carries his Cross
5. Jesus Dies on the Cross

The Five Glorious Mysteries
   (Traditionally Prayed on Wednesdays and Sundays)
1. The Resurrection of Jesus from the Dead
2. The Ascension of Jesus into Heaven
3. The Gift of the Holy Spirit on Pentecost
4. The Assumption of Mary into Heaven
5. The Crowning of Mary as Queen

As we said earlier, these mysteries cover the entire life of Christ, from his conception in the womb of his mother Mary to his entry into glory through his resurrection, ascension, and his sending the Holy Spirit. The mysteries of Jesus therefore cover our entire lives as well. They are storehouses of graces for every moment and every circumstance of our lives, from our conception to our own entry into glory. In fact, they are our pathways to glory. Every time we pray the rosary, or a part of it, we make a little part of our journey with Jesus and help others along their journey as well.

The Rosary, a Christ-centered Prayer

As we contemplate all these mysteries of Christ, we can see very clearly how the rosary is a Christ-centered prayer. Pope John Paul II accentuated this in his apostolic letter on the Rosary when he said: "The Rosary, though clearly Marian in character, is at heart a Christocentric prayer. In the sobriety of its elements, it has all the *depth of the Gospel message in its entirety*, of which it can be said to be a compendium."[16]

What then do we say about the last two Glorious Mysteries of the rosary, which commemorate the Assumption of Mary into heaven (the fourth Glorious Mystery) and her being crowned as Queen of Heaven (fifth Glorious Mystery)? How do these fit in a "Christocentric" prayer? They fit precisely as they show forth in a most wonderful manner the completed work of Jesus—not only in the person of Mary (which they do in the first instance), but also in his Church (of which Mary is an exemplar), and indeed in all of creation.

In these last two mysteries of the rosary, God as it were, shows forth the perfection of His Son's work of salvation. He proclaims to all the world, "See what my Son has done for you! See the 'eternal redemption' (Heb. 9:12) my Son has obtained for you. See the 'eternal weight of glory beyond all comparison' (II Cor. 4:17) that is stored up for you in heaven. The glory you see in Mary, you will one day see in the Church and in all of my creation."[17]

These last two Glorious Mysteries indeed bring the rosary to a crescendo of praise. "Praised be Jesus for accomplishing for us so great a salvation! Praised be the Father for loving us so much, for sending his Son, and for "the riches of glory in his inheritance among the holy ones" (Eph.

---

16   Apostolic Letter *Rosarium Virginis Mariae* of the Supreme Pontiff John Paul II to the Bishops, Clergy and Faithful on the Most Holy Rosary, 1 (Introduction).

17   See Paul's statement about the glory of creation in Romans 8:21.

1:18)! And praised be the Holy Spirit who from the conception of Jesus until Pentecost brought God to earth and who now fills the universe with God's glory! "Holy, holy, holy is the Lord of hosts...All the earth is filled with his glory!" (Is. 6:3).

Do these last two mysteries of the rosary glorify God? Indeed they do, in a most wonderful way.

CHAPTER 6

SUGGESTIONS FOR PRAYING THE TWENTY MYSTERIES

There are several ways you can use this part of the book.

A. Praying the Rosary

This book is first and foremost a PRAYER BOOK. It is to be used *as you pray the rosary*. At the same time, you will notice that I have included more material with each mystery than you could easily use as you pray the mystery. For this reason I suggest that you be selective as you pray the rosary and use those parts and those petitions that will be most conducive to your prayer.

The following are some suggestions:

(1) After announcing each mystery, you could select one of the petitions that are given and announce that petition. This would be the prayer intention for that decade. This would be the simplest way to use the material given for each mystery. You

will notice that with some prayer intentions, provision is made to mention the name of a particular person—or persons—for whom you wish to pray. This is provided in the text with an underline. But you may also wish to mention particular names even where this underline is not provided. Other optional parts of petitions are indicated by parentheses (   ).

(2) For each mystery at least ten petitions are listed. If you wish, you could announce one petition for each "Hail Mary."

(3) Preceding some of the petitions is a description of one or several of the blessings that Jesus has obtained for us through that mystery. This description could also be read as an introduction to the petition.

(4) At the beginning of most mysteries there is an introduction, which gives a condensed description of the mystery. If you wish, you could read this introduction—or part of it—after you announce the mystery. You could then, if you wish, continue with any of the suggestions as given above in (1), (2), or (3).

B. A Prayerful Reading of each Mystery

At your leisure you can read through each mystery and ponder its many riches. During this time of prayerful reading ("*lectio divina*")[18], ask God in your own words for these blessings for yourselves and for others. Spend as much time as you wish with each petition. You may even wish to take one petition as your prayer intention for an entire day.

---

18   This Latin expression is pronounced: LEX-ee-o dee-VEE-nah, and means simply "divine reading." Your reading of the mysteries will become "divine reading" when, as you read the scriptures and the prayer intentions for each mystery, you let prayer flow from your heart by the leading of the Holy Spirit.

Becoming acquainted with each mystery in this way will also help you pray these mysteries with more meaning when you pray the rosary.

C. Bible Studies

The scriptures listed for each mystery could be used for a series of bible studies for that mystery. I would suggest that you choose approximately 5-10 scriptures for each bible study.[19] After reading each scripture— either in a group or privately—ask the following questions for each scripture passage:

1. What are the blessings that this scripture reveals that Jesus has obtained for us (for me)?
2. How can we (I) best obtain these blessings and live them out in our (my) daily lives (life)?

---

19   For additional bible studies you may also wish to use the scriptures listed here and there in Parts I and III of this book.

CHAPTER 7

THE JOYFUL MYSTERIES

The Joyful Mysteries of the rosary present to us five very important events in the life of Jesus from his Conception to the end of his hidden life. These events are:

1. The Annunciation to Mary of the Incarnation
2. The Visitation of Mary to Elizabeth
3. The Birth of Jesus
4. The Presentation of the Child Jesus in the Temple
5. The Finding of Jesus in the Temple

A special character of **joy** pervades all these mysteries. This joy was announced by the angel at Jesus' birth, "I proclaim to you good news of great joy that will be for all the people" (Lk. 2:10). God's gift of joy awaits us as we pray these mysteries!

Besides the five particular events of the Joyful Mysteries, there are also a number of other very significant events closely connected with them. I mention these with each joyful mystery where this is appropriate.

For example, with the mystery of the Annunciation I have included the Immaculate Conception of Mary since it is so intimately connected to the Conception of Jesus. The Book of Wisdom tells us that God's wisdom does not dwell "in a body under debt of sin" (Wis. 1:4). How then could God's Wisdom, God's eternal Word, take flesh from Mary's body if it were ever "under debt of sin"—even the generational sin of Adam (Original Sin)?

With the Birth of Jesus I have added the Adoration of the Magi, which the Church celebrates on the feast of the Epiphany.

With the mystery of the Presentation of the Child Jesus in the Temple, I have added the Circumcision of Jesus, which St. Luke mentions immediately before the Presentation. This is significant for a number of reasons. By accepting the sign of the covenant that God made with Abraham, Jesus is declared to be the inheritor of these promises. At that moment "he was named Jesus, the name given him by the angel before he was conceived in the womb" (Lk. 2:21). I have also joined to this mystery the Flight into Egypt and the Massacre of the Infants as related in the gospel of Matthew 2:13-18. Because the mystery of the Presentation stands at the beginning of Jesus' childhood, it is appropriate in this mystery to pray for children and to draw from this mystery the graces needed for the healing of our own childhood.

The mystery of the Finding of Jesus in the Temple marks Jesus' transition from childhood to adulthood. And so in this mystery we pray especially for young people to be given the grace to make this transition with Jesus through the Holy Spirit. This mystery also marks the beginning of the entire hidden life of Jesus covering approximately 18 years of his life. These years are also the source of many graces for those many events of our lives that are hidden, ordinary, and seemingly unimportant. In this mystery we also remember the Holy Family and pray for the graces needed today by all families.

Even though we call these mysteries "joyful," they also make us aware that the lives of Jesus, Mary, and Joseph were even then filled with pain and sorrow. I thought it important to bring this out since it so clearly reflects the reality of the lives of so many children and their parents. How many children today are suffering terrible pain! This pain needs to be healed through the pains of Jesus' infancy and childhood. And how many parents are suffering anguish because of their children! Mary and Joseph can bring them strength and comfort.

The Church has traditionally commemorated the "Seven Sorrows of the Blessed Virgin Mary." The first three of these fall within the Joyful Mysteries. They are: The Prophecy of Simeon, The Flight into Egypt, and The Loss of Jesus in Jerusalem.[20]

---

20   For the list of these Seven Sorrows see pages 91-92.

THE ANNUNCIATION TO MARY OF THE INCARNATION

Luke 1:26-38; Matthew 1:18-25; John 1:1-14; Colossians 1:15-20; 2:9; Hebrews 1:1-4; I John 1:1-3; Proverbs 8:22-36; Sirach 24:1-12; Wisdom 7:22-8:1.

The word "Annunciation" does not name the mystery, but rather describes the activity of the angel Gabriel who *announces* the mystery. The mystery which Gabriel announces is the mystery of the **Incarnation**: God's incredible gift—that the Second Person of the Blessed Trinity (God the Son) unites himself to our human nature in Jesus Christ, who is both fully God and fully man.

We will contemplate this mystery forever in heaven and it will be one of the greatest joys of heaven. Yet we will never completely grasp its full nature.

Before all else, this mystery invites us to pray this decade of the rosary in thanksgiving. And so we pray
- **in thanksgiving to God the Father for giving us his Son** (John 3:16).
- **[in thanksgiving] to God the Son for becoming human for us and for emptying himself of glory to assume the condition of a slave** (Phil. 2:7).
- **[in thanksgiving] to God the Holy Spirit for accomplishing the mystery of the Incarnation in the womb of the Virgin Mary** (Lk. 1:35).
- **[in thanksgiving] to the Blessed Virgin Mary for giving her "Yes" to God.**
- **[in thanksgiving] to St. Joseph for being the faithful husband of Mary and loving foster father of Jesus.**

The conception of Jesus heralded the fulfillment of Isaiah's prophecy: "Behold, the virgin shall be with child and bear a son, and they shall name him Emmanuel," a name which means "God is with us" (Mt. 1:23). And so we pray

- **that we might know that Jesus is forever "Emmanuel" and is always with us.**

Through the Incarnation of the Son of God, "the light shines in the darkness and the darkness has not overcome it" (John 1:5). And so we pray

- **that those who live in darkness will be filled with the light of Jesus.**

In this mystery we recall that by becoming man, Jesus also joined himself to every part of our human nature and to every moment of our lives. And so in this decade we pray

- **that every part of our human nature and every moment of our lives will be united to Jesus.**

By joining our own conception to the conception of Jesus, we can receive a root healing—a healing at the first moment of our conception—and so receive a healing of the effects of Original Sin. To receive this grace we ask the intercession of Mary through her Immaculate Conception. Mary's conception was joined fully to the conception of her Son and so from the first moment of her conception she was preserved from the stain of Original Sin. Mary's body was never under the power of sin. It always belonged to God in a full and total way. See Wisdom 1:4 and I Corinthians 6:13b. And so as we pray this decade of the rosary,

- **we thank God for the grace of Mary's Immaculate Conception.**
- **we pray that our own conception be joined to the conception of Jesus—so that the very first moment of our existence will be made holy. We pray this same grace for _____.**
- **for the healing of the sins of rebellion and of disobedience which we have inherited from our first parents.**

48

- that all babies in the womb may be united to Jesus during the time he was in the womb of his mother Mary and so be sanctified and consecrated to God.

In this mystery we pray
- for the prevention of abortions and that God will put into the hearts of mothers the same sentiments for their children that were in the heart of Mary as she carried the child Jesus.
- for babies who will be aborted—for their sanctification and that they will be filled with the Holy Spirit in the wombs of their mothers.

Mary believed when the angel Gabriel told her that she would conceive the Son of God by the Holy Spirit and that Elizabeth had conceived in her old age. She believed that "nothing will be impossible for God" (Lk. 1:37). And so we pray
- that we will have the faith of Mary to believe that "nothing will be impossible for God" and so receive the answer to the prayer we now offer to God: _____.

Through the mystery of the Incarnation we pray
- that we may become one body and one spirit with Jesus and so share mystically in his Incarnation (I Cor. 6:15,17; 12:27).
- that God will bestow on us the holiness of Mary so that the Word may become flesh in us.
- that like Mary we may be "full of grace" and pleasing to God in every way.
- that we may always offer ourselves to God as his humble servants and say with Mary, "May it be done to me according to your word" (Lk. 1:38).
- that Mary will obtain for us the grace to say a full and complete "Yes" to God for whatever God's will may be for our lives, so that, like Mary, we will be God's instruments in bringing Jesus to the world.

We pray
- **for those who do not yet know Jesus as the Eternal Son of God, that the Holy Spirit will bring them the revelation of this truth.**

By his Incarnation, the Son of God united all of creation to himself. He will also one day set creation "free from slavery to corruption" to "share in the glorious freedom of the children of God" (Rom. 8:21). And so we pray
- **that we might honor and reverence all of God's creation and be good stewards of God's wonderful gifts (Gen. 2:15).**

As an act of faith you may conclude this decade of the rosary by praying:
We thank you, Father, for giving us the grace we have asked for through this holy mystery.

You may wish to add your own intentions below.

THE VISITATION OF MARY TO ELIZABETH

Luke 1:39-56.

"During those days Mary set out and traveled to the hill country in haste to a town of Judah, where she entered the house of Zechariah and greeted Elizabeth (Lk. 1:39-40).

Mary was the first missionary. God sent her to announce the good news that the Son of God had come in the flesh. "How beautiful on the mountains are the feet of him [her] who brings glad tidings, announcing peace, bearing good news, announcing salvation" (Is. 52:7). In this decade of the rosary, we pray
 • **that through the intercession of Mary, the whole Church will be renewed in its mission to spread the good news about Jesus, and that we will make haste to do so as Mary did.**

Both Mary and Elizabeth fostered the life within their wombs with great love and care. And so in this decade we pray for pregnant mothers. We pray
 • **that pregnant mothers will have all the help they need to bring their children to full term, that God will send people to encourage them and assist them with their needs.**
 • **that like Elizabeth, pregnant mothers will receive a visitation from Mary—that our Blessed Mother will be with them throughout the term of their pregnancy.**

Mary was thoughtful and attentive to Elizabeth in her needs. And so we pray

- **that like Mary we will always be attentive to those who need our help.**

Mary brought to Elizabeth and John the presence of Jesus and the Holy Spirit. They were both filled with the Holy Spirit through Mary's visit (Luke 1:15b,41). Mary always brings Jesus and the Holy Spirit with her. And so we pray in this mystery

- **that Mary will visit us and bring us Jesus and a new infilling of the Holy Spirit. We pray this grace also for _____.**
- **that Mary will visit the Church, our parish, our world—to bring Jesus and the Holy Spirit to all people.**
- **that like Mary we may be bearers of Christ and the Holy Spirit and so bring Jesus and the Holy Spirit to others.**

Mary brought blessing to the infant John in the womb of Elizabeth. He was "filled with the Holy Spirit" (Lk. 1:15) and leaped for joy (Lk. 1:44). And so we pray

- **that Mary will visit all unborn children in the wombs of their mothers so that these children may be blessed, sanctified, healed, and protected from all evil.**
- **that our own time in the wombs of our mothers will be healed, made holy, and be filled with the Holy Spirit by encountering Jesus as did John the Baptist. We pray this grace also for _____.**

Elizabeth recognized Mary as the "Mother of my Lord." And so we pray

- **that all people will recognize and honor Mary as the Mother of God.**

Elizabeth also recognized that Mary was blessed because she believed that what was spoken to her by the Lord would be fulfilled (Lk. 1:45).

And so we pray
- that through Mary's intercession we will believe in all of God's promises and so see them fulfilled in our lives.

On the occasion of her Visitation, Mary prayed her beautiful prayer, the Magnificat. And so
- **we ask Mary to teach us how to praise God from our hearts as she did.**

We also pray
- that our souls will always proclaim "the greatness of the Lord" (Lk. 1:46).
- that with Mary our spirits will rejoice in God our savior (Lk. 1:47).
- that we might call Mary "blessed" and be blessed with her by our obedience to the Father (Lk. 1:48).
- that with Mary we might recognize the great things the "Mighty One" has done for us and call his name holy (Lk. 1:49; Mt. 6:9).
- that we might always have a reverential fear of God and so receive his divine mercy (Lk. 1:50).
- that Mary would teach us how to be humble in mind and heart and so be lifted up by God (Lk. 1:51-52).
- that God would fill with good things those who are both spiritually and physically hungry (Lk. 1:53).
- that God will remember his mercy and come to the help of all of his children (especially for _____) (Lk. 1:54).

(You may wish to pray the Magnificat at the conclusion of this decade or at the conclusion of the Joyful Mysteries.)

As an act of faith you may conclude this decade of the rosary by praying:
We thank you, Father, for giving us the grace we have asked for through this holy mystery.

You may wish to add your own intentions below.

THE BIRTH OF JESUS

Luke 2:1-20; Matthew 1:18-2:18; Galatians 4:4-7; Titus 3:4-7; Philippians 2:6-8.

Jesus is the "firstborn among many brothers [and sisters]" (Rom. 8:29).

And so we pray
- **that our birth will be joined to the birth of Jesus and so be healed and made holy.**

At the birth of Jesus there was great rejoicing (Lk. 2:10-14) both in heaven and on earth, and so we pray
- **that we will experience the joy of God the Father and the celebration of all heaven at our birth.**
- **that any rejection we may have experienced at our birth be healed by our sharing in the birth of Jesus.**

"On coming into the world, Jesus said: "Sacrifice and offering you did not desire, but a body you have prepared for me; holocausts and sin offerings you took no delight in. Then I said, 'As is written of me in the book, I have come to do your will, O God'" (Heb. 10:5-7). Jesus fully embraced the will of his Father to come into the world and to give his life in sacrifice for the world's salvation. He "rejoiced like a champion to run his course" (Ps. 19:6). We pray
- **for the grace to embrace our lives fully according to the will of the Father so that with Jesus we too will say from our hearts, "I have come to do your will, O God" and will rejoice like champions to run the course of our lives.**

Jesus was born so that we might be born again as children of God and so enter the Kingdom of God. (See John 3:3-8; John 1:1-13.) And so we pray

- **that through the birth of Jesus and the intercession of Mary, we might be born again with Jesus as children of God and so enter the radiant life of God's kingdom. We pray this grace for _____.**

God has given us the assurance that we are his children by sending "the spirit of his Son into our hearts, crying out, 'Abba, Father!'" (Gal. 4:6). And so we pray

- **that through the birth of Jesus, we might know God as our loving Father and call him our "Abba" in the Holy Spirit."**

Jesus said, "I assure you, unless you change and become like little children you will not enter the kingdom of God" (Mt. 18:3). And so we pray

- **for the grace to relate to God always as a little child together with Jesus.**
- **for the grace to know Mary as our Mother and to relate to her as her little children as did Jesus.**
- **for the grace to love Jesus as did his Mother Mary and St. Joseph.**
- **that mothers and fathers will love their children as Mary and Joseph loved Jesus.**

At the birth of Jesus the angels announced peace on earth (Lk. 2:14). They announced the birth of the child who was the "Prince of Peace" (Is. 9:5), who would teach the world how to "beat their swords into ploughshares and their spears into pruning hooks" (Is. 2:4) so that nations would not "train for war again" (Is. 2:4). And so we pray in this mystery

- **that Jesus, the Prince of Peace, would reign over all hearts and over all the nations of the world to establish his Kingdom of peace.**

Jesus was born in poverty. Mary laid him in a manger, "because there was no room for them in the inn" (Lk. 2:7). Jesus lived in poverty. "Foxes have dens and birds of the sky have nests, but the Son of Man has nowhere to rest his head" (Lk. 9:58). Jesus died in poverty. "He emptied himself" (Phil. 2:7). And so we pray

- **for those who are poor, that we and others will be good stewards of God's riches to provide for their needs** (Tobit 4:7; Sir. 4:1-10; I Tim. 6:17-19).
- **that we will "guard against all greed" (Lk. 12:15), trust God to provide for what we need, and be content with what God provides for us** (Lk. 12:22-34; I Tim. 6:6-10,17-19).

In this ineffable mystery we also celebrate the EPIPHANY of Jesus. God manifested his Son not only to the Jewish people in fulfillment of God's promises, but also to the Gentiles (all non-Jewish people) beginning with the three Magi who came from the east, following the guidance of the Christmas star. Paul spoke of this mystery when he said that "the Gentiles are coheirs, members of the same body, and copartners in the promise in Christ Jesus through the gospel" (Eph. 3:6). And so in this mystery we pray

- **that God would grant EVERYONE on earth the light of a new Epiphany, revealing Jesus to them as his eternal Son, the long-awaited Messiah and Savior of the whole world. We pray this grace especially for _____.**

The Magi offered Jesus gifts of gold, frankincense, and myrrh. And so we pray

- **that we will follow the example of the Magi and offer our gifts generously to God and to God's people.**

Jesus came into this world to offer himself as a gift to us. He came "not to be served, but to serve and to give his life as a ransom for many" (Mk. 10:45). And so we pray

- **that with Jesus we might seek "not to be served, but to serve" and to give our lives as a gift to God for the salvation of souls.**

As an act of faith you may conclude this decade of the rosary by praying:
We thank you, Father, for giving us the grace we have asked for through this holy mystery.

You may wish to add your own intentions below.

THE PRESENTATION OF THE CHILD JESUS IN THE TEMPLE

Luke 2:22-38; Exodus 13:1-16.

By presenting the infant Jesus to God in the temple, Mary and Joseph fulfilled God's command for this Rite of Consecration. God told his people: "Consecrate to me every first-born...both of man and beast, for it belongs to me" (Ex. 13:2). The consecration of the first-born was a sign that the WHOLE PEOPLE belonged to God. They belonged to God because God had delivered them from their slavery in Egypt. We now belong to God because Jesus has redeemed us from our slavery to sin and to Satan and has consecrated us to himself as his holy people.

And so through this mystery we pray
- **that all parents will consecrate their children to God—through Baptism and through other prayers of consecration.**

In this mystery
- **we join Mary and Joseph in bringing all children to God, consecrating them to God together with Jesus. We consecrate all children also to Jesus and to Mary.**
- **that our childhood years might be consecrated to God and so be sanctified and healed through the childhood of Jesus.**

Simeon and Anna[21] were faithful to God through many years of patient waiting. We pray

- **for the grace to persevere in our faith, knowing that one day "our eyes will see the Savior." We pray for others to persevere in their faith—especially those who may be discouraged by the sufferings and hurts of their lives.**

We also pray with Simeon

- **that the light of Jesus will in fact enlighten all the nations of the earth and that everyone will receive the light of faith to know Jesus.**

Simeon told Mary that "this child is destined for the fall and rise of many in Israel, and to be a sign that will be contradicted" (Lk. 2:34) and that her own soul would be pierced by a sword (Lk. 2:35). In this mystery we pray

- **for all mothers who feel the sufferings of their children and share their pains and sorrows, that they will be comforted by the Mother of Jesus.[22]**

Besides being presented in the temple, the child Jesus was also circumcised on the eighth day (Lk. 2:21). By his circumcision, Jesus signified that he was a descendant of Abraham and was the heir of the promises God made to Abraham (Gen. 15:5-6,18-21; 17:9-14; Gal. 3:16). Jesus would also fulfill these promises in a far greater way. And so we pray

- **that through the mystery of Jesus' circumcision, we will inherit eternal life and all the covenant promises God has made to his people.**

---

21   Read the passage in the gospel of Luke about Simeon and Anna: Luke 2:25-38. God had promised Simeon "that he should not see death before he had seen the Messiah of the Lord" (Lk. 2:26). The prophetess Anna had served God faithfully for many years. "She never left the temple, but worshiped night and day with fasting and prayer" (Lk. 2:37).

22   This petition is based on one of the seven sorrows of Mary.

The baptism of infants fulfills the ancient rite of circumcision. And so we pray

- **that all children will receive the sacrament of baptism and thus become children of God and heirs of all God's promises.**

At his circumcision Jesus shed his blood for the first time. And so we pray

- **for all infants and children who suffer, that their pains will be healed through the sufferings of Jesus.**

At his circumcision Jesus was given his name "Jesus" (Lk. 2:21). And so we pray

- **that everyone will call on the name of Jesus and be saved (Rom.10:13).**
- **that everyone will hold the name of Jesus in great respect and honor (Ex. 20:7; Phil. 2:10).**
- **in reparation for the many times that the name of Jesus is used in vain.**

Mary and Joseph had to flee with the child Jesus to Egypt in order to save his life (Mt. 2:13-15). And so we pray

- **for all refugees and for all who are persecuted for the sake of righteousness (Mt. 5:10).[23]**

In his attempt to kill Jesus, Herod had many innocent children slaughtered. And so we pray

- **for all innocent children who are killed through abortion and for all children who are abused, abandoned, and neglected.**

As an act of faith you may conclude this decade of the rosary by praying:

---

23   This petition is based on one of the seven sorrows of Mary.

We thank you, Father, for giving us the grace we have asked for through this holy mystery.

You may wish to add your own intentions below.

THE FINDING OF JESUS
IN THE TEMPLE

Luke 2:41-52.

In this mystery we see Jesus as a young man at the age of 12, moving from childhood to adulthood. This time of transition in a person's life is very crucial and also very difficult. Jesus makes this transition in life so that our own young adult years may be healed and made whole. And so we pray

- **that Jesus would heal all areas of our young adult years that need to be healed (especially _____).**

As a young man "Jesus advanced in wisdom and age and favor before God and man" (Lk. 2:52). And so we pray

- **that through this mystery all young people will advance "in wisdom and age and favor before God and man" (Lk. 2:52).**

In this mystery we see Jesus, Mary, and Joseph going to Jerusalem to celebrate the feast of Passover. In doing so they give an example to all families to worship God together. And so we pray

- **that all families will worship God together, both in church and in their homes.**

As a young man, Jesus hears and follows the call of God for his life. He knows he must be in his Father's house, doing his Father's will. And so we pray

- **for all young people, that they will hear and follow the call of God for their lives.**

64

Jesus followed God's call even when his parents did not understand. And so we pray

- **that young people will have the strength and courage to break away from unhealthy human attachments, peer pressure, and other people's expectations in order to follow God's call for their lives.**

Mary and Joseph did not fully understand God's plan for Jesus, but they surrendered him to God and pondered God's purposes for their child. Parents likewise do not know all that God has in store for their children. And so we pray in this mystery

- **that parents will let go of unhealthy control over their children's lives and will pray that God's will, not their own, will be done in their children.**

Mary and Joseph experienced much pain at losing Jesus. Many parents today have lost their children through kidnapping, through children running away from home, joining cults, or through a breakdown of communication. And so we pray

- **for parents who have lost their children, that their children might be found and that all hurts in relationships with them will be healed.**[24]

In the temple Jesus studied and pondered the Word of God and listened to the teaching of his elders (Lk. 2:46). We pray

- **that young people will have a desire to learn the Word of God and will listen respectfully to the teachings of their parents and elders** (Sir. 6:32-37).
- **for parents and teachers that they will faithfully teach God's Word to their children** (Deut. 6:7; Ps. 78:4-7).

---

24   This petition is based on one of the seven sorrows of Mary.

- **for the teachers and administrators of our schools (especially _____ School), that they be guided by the wisdom and truth of the Holy Spirit.**

Jesus shows respect for his elders and offers obedience to his parents. "He went down with them then, and came to Nazareth, and was obedient to them" (Luke 2:51). And so we pray

- **that children will show respect to their parents and give them loving obedience.**

We pray

- **for young people who are alienated from their parents, that they will be reconciled.** (Mal. 3:24; Lk. 1:17)

We pray for all troubled young people, especially

- **for runaway and homeless children.**
- **for children who are used and abused by others, especially through pornography.**
- **for youth who have no wise adults to guide them.**
- **for young people who rebel against the wisdom of the adults in their lives.**
- **for youth who do not know Jesus, who are caught up in drugs, alcohol, pornography, gangs, and other destructive habits.**
- **for young adults who are depressed, who live without meaning, and who are tempted to suicide.**
- **for young people who are being drawn into witchcraft and other occult practices.**
- **that Jesus would set all young people free, save them, and heal them.**

At this time in a young person's life there is the emergence of the powers of sexuality. In his human nature Jesus integrated his sexuality perfectly and enables us to do the same. And so we pray

- for young people who are caught in unhealthy sexual practices, especially premarital sex and pornography.
- for young people who are confused about their sexual orientation, that God would heal them and guide them to a healthy heterosexual orientation.

Jesus, Mary, and Joseph present us with the model of a holy family. And so we pray

- for all families, that through the intercession of the Holy Family, they may live together in love, peace, respect for one another, and in mutual service. We pray especially for the family of _____.

Jesus' life was hidden for many years. He served God and others without attracting any attention to himself.[25] And so we pray

- that we might serve God and others in humility, without seeking recognition or reward.

As an act of faith you may conclude this decade of the rosary by praying:
We thank you, Father, for giving us the grace we have asked for through this holy mystery.

You may wish to add your own intentions below.

---

25   Recall Jesus' teaching about this in Matthew 6:1-8 and 16-18. We should not even take notice of our own good deeds: "When you give alms, do not let your left hand know what your right is doing" (Mt. 6:3).

CHAPTER 8

THE LUMINOUS MYSTERIES

In 2002 Pope John Paul II wrote his Apostolic Letter *The Rosary of the Virgin Mary.* In this Letter the Holy Father chose five mysteries from the public life of Jesus to be commemorated in the Rosary. He called these mysteries the "Luminous Mysteries." These mysteries are:

1. The Baptism of Jesus in the Jordan
2. The Wedding Feast at Cana
3. The Proclamation of the Kingdom of God
4. The Transfiguration of Jesus
5. The Institution of the Holy Eucharist

It was especially appropriate that these mysteries be called "luminous" mysteries—mysteries of light. Of these mysteries, the most clearly "luminous" mystery is the Transfiguration of Jesus in which his whole person shines with the light of God's glory. But we also see this light at Jesus' Baptism and when he began to proclaim the Kingdom of God. Matthew sees these two events as the fulfillment of the prophecy of Isaiah, "the people who sit in darkness have seen a great light" (Mt. 4:16). John also tells us that, at the wedding feast at Cana, Jesus "revealed his glory" (John 2:11). And with the Institution of the Eucharist, Jesus assures us that we will continue to have in our midst him who is the Light of the World (John 8:12; 9:5). These mysteries are indeed "luminous."

Together with these five Luminous Mysteries I have also mentioned a number of other important events from Jesus' public ministry that are intimately connected with them.

With the Baptism of Jesus I have included Jesus' Temptation in the desert.

With the Proclamation of the Kingdom of God I have made mention of Jesus' choice of the 12 apostles and his establishing Peter at the head of the apostles.

With the Transfiguration I have included Jesus' predictions of his passion, death, and resurrection. In the gospels of Matthew, Mark, and Luke these predictions immediately precede the Transfiguration, indicating their close connection with this mystery.

Other events closely associated with the Last Supper that I have included are the following:
1. Jesus washes the feet of his disciples.
2. Jesus inaugurates the New Covenant with its new commandment.
3. Jesus institutes the ministerial priesthood.
4. Jesus prays his high-priestly prayer.

The Luminous Mysteries are rich with God's blessings. Let us pray them with great faith.

THE BAPTISM OF JESUS
IN THE JORDAN

Matthew 3:13-17; Mark 1:9-11; Luke 3:21-22; John 1:29-34.

The Baptism of Jesus anticipates the mystery of the cross. Jesus is the innocent Lamb of God (John 1:29) who takes on himself all the sins of the world in order to wash them away in his precious Blood and atone for them with his heavenly Father. As Paul says, "For our sake he made him to be sin who did not know sin, so that we might become the righteousness of God in him" (II Cor. 5:21). That is why Jesus insists that John baptize him—not to wash away his own sins, but to wash away the sins of the world. This is also why Jesus says that "it is fitting for us to fulfill ALL righteousness" (Mt. 3:15). [Emphasis added] Jesus will wash away ALL sins and will make up for ALL that is lacking in EVERY person's life. And so in this mystery we pray
- **in thanksgiving to Jesus for taking on himself the burden of our sins, for washing them away, and for fulfilling all that is lacking in our righteousness before the Father. (We thank Jesus for doing this for _____.)**
- **for all who are preparing to be baptized (especially for _____), for those who are helping to prepare them, and for their sponsors.**

As the people came to be baptized, they confessed their sins. And so in this mystery we pray
- **for the grace to be truly sorry for all our sins.**
- **for the conversion of all sinners, especially those who are dying.**
- **for the grace of conversion for _____.**
- **for the grace to make a sincere confession of our sins.**

At his baptism Jesus was anointed and filled with the Holy Spirit. "He saw the Spirit of God descending like a dove and coming upon him" (Mt. 3:16). And so John said of Jesus, "he will baptize you with the Holy Spirit and fire" (Mt. 3:11). In this mystery therefore we pray

- **that Jesus will baptize us in "the Holy Spirit and in fire" as well as those for whom we pray, especially _____ .**

At his baptism Jesus heard the voice of the Father saying, "This is my beloved Son, with whom I am well pleased" (Mt. 3:17). And so we pray

- **that through the grace of our baptism we will be able to hear the Father say to us, "You are my beloved son/ my beloved daughter" and be able to live always as God's beloved sons and daughters.**

As Christians we were baptized "in the name of the Father, and of the Son, and of the Holy Spirit." And so we pray

- **that we will know and love each person of the Blessed Trinity in a personal and intimate way.**

In order to fulfill the Father's plan for his life, Jesus had to leave his life in Nazareth with his mother, his relatives, and his friends. Mary also had to let go of her Son. And so we pray

- **for the grace to leave everything in order to follow God's will for our lives.**
- **for Mary's intercession for parents that they will be able to let go of their children and will encourage them to follow God's will for their lives.**

Whenever God bestows special graces on people, the devil tries to steal these graces away. This was true for Jesus as well. At his baptism, Jesus was empowered by the Holy Spirit and strengthened by the voice of his Father for his mission as Savior of the world. Satan was there to try to rob Jesus of this empowerment. But through his baptism, Jesus is prepared to do battle against Satan and all Satan's temptations. Through prayer and fasting, and by wielding the "sword of the Spirit which is the Word of God" (Eph. 6:17), Jesus won the victory over Satan and all his deceptions (Mt. 4:1-11; Lk. 4:1-13). And so we pray

- **that through the power of the Holy Spirit working in us, we will win the victory over all Satan's temptations and deceptions.**
- **that through our knowledge and confession of God's word, we will overcome all the temptations of the devil.**

Jesus' baptism marked the beginning of his public ministry. In this mystery he shows us how we too are to prepare ourselves to minister to others. And so we pray

- **for those who are in positions of authority and power, that they will prepare themselves for their ministry by repentance, submission to the will of God, and by being empowered by the Holy Spirit.**

As an act of faith you may conclude this decade of the rosary by praying:
We thank you, Father, for giving us the grace we have asked for through this holy mystery.

You may wish to add your own intentions below.

THE WEDDING FEAST AT CANA

John 2:1-11.

The wedding at Cana announces and prefigures another and greater wedding: the Wedding Feast of the Lamb and his bride, the Church (Rev. 19:7-9). This wedding will take place when Jesus' hour has come. As Jesus hung on the cross, he poured out an overflowing abundance of the new wine of his precious Blood. At the same time John tells us "he handed over the Spirit" (John 19:30). His precious Blood and his gift of the Holy Spirit possess and convey the infinite love of the heart of Jesus for his bride, the Church, and for each one of us. The mother of Jesus is present at this wedding. She is instrumental in obtaining for us this "new wine." She knows her Son and gently urges him to do what is necessary to obtain this "wine" for us. She will even encourage him to go to the cross for us.

At the Wedding Feast at Cana Jesus blesses all weddings and all marriages whenever he is invited, and so we pray
- **for the healing of all marriages (especially the marriage of _____), that they will be blessed and made holy by the presence of Jesus and his Mother.**

We pray
- **that husbands and wives will have an abundance of the new wine of the Holy Spirit with which to love one another and to love their children.**

We pray

- **for those marriages in particular that are in trouble, that Jesus and Mary will bring them God's divine love and peace.**
- **for those marriages that are not blessed by the Church, that both husband and wife will seek this blessing and will seek to live according to God's holy will.**
- **for those marriages that have ended in divorce, that Jesus with his Mother will show the way to healing, reconciliation, and forgiveness.**
- **for single parents and for their children, that they will experience the presence of Jesus and Mary with them and will trust in God to provide for all their needs.**

We pray

- **for those who are being called to the married life, that they will invite Jesus and his Mother to take charge of all their preparations, and in particular the choice of the right marriage partner.**

The wedding at Cana announces the eternal Wedding Feast of the Lamb. "Let us rejoice and be glad and give him glory. For the wedding day of the Lamb has come, his bride has made herself ready. She was allowed to wear a bright, clean linen garment. (The linen represents the righteous deeds of the holy ones.) (Rev. 19:7-8)." And so we pray

- **that through the graces of her Immaculate and undivided Heart, Mary will prepare us, and the whole Church, for the eternal Wedding Feast of the Lamb.**
- **that all our sins will be washed away in the Blood of Jesus, that our "robes" will be made pure and without stain.**
- **that even in this life we will experience our "mystical marriage" with Jesus.**

We pray
- **for the Church, the beloved bride of Christ, that Jesus will "present to himself the church in splendor, without spot or wrinkle or any such thing, that she might be holy and without blemish"** (Eph. 5:17).

We pray
- **that we will know God's jealous love for us as his bride, and that our thoughts may never be corrupted from a sincere and pure commitment to Christ.** (See II Corinthians 11:2-3.)

Mary tells the servants at the wedding feast, "Do whatever he tells you." And so we pray through Mary's intercession
- **for the grace to do whatever Jesus tells us.**

The Wedding at Cana announces that the fulfillment of all human love lies in the love of God which overflows from the heart of Jesus and is poured into our hearts through the Holy Spirit (Rom. 5:5). And so we pray
- **that we will seek the fulfillment of our need for love in the heart of Jesus and in the gift of the Holy Spirit.**
- **that through her intercession, Mary will obtain for us the New Wine of the Holy Spirit.**

Jesus sanctifies sexual love in marriage and gives us the grace to direct our sexuality in ways that are pleasing to him. And so we pray
- **that our sexuality will be made holy in Jesus and that Jesus will set free all those who are caught in sexual sins, especially adultery, fornication, and pornography.**
- **for the healing of those who through homosexuality miss the blessings of marriage.**

As an act of faith you may conclude this decade of the rosary by praying:

We thank you, Father, for giving us the grace we have asked for through this holy mystery.

You may wish to add your own intentions below.

THE PROCLAMATION OF THE KINGDOM OF GOD

Matthew 4:17,23-24; 10:7-8; 11:4-5; Mark 1:14-15,32-34; Luke 4:14-19,40-41.

Jesus not only proclaimed the Kingdom of God; he made it present, so that even now we can enter into it. Jesus proclaimed the Kingdom of God in four primary ways: 1) through preaching and teaching, 2) through the forgiveness of sins, 3) through healing, and 4) through deliverance from evil spirits. See Matthew 10:7-8 and Luke 24:47.

Jesus proclaimed the Kingdom of God by his preaching. He called all people to enter God's Kingdom through repentance and faith (Mk. 1:15). He also chose 12 apostles and 72 other disciples (representing the whole Church) to continue his proclamation of the Kingdom. And so, through this mystery of the rosary, we pray

- **for the preaching ministry of the Church, especially for bishops, priests, and deacons that they will proclaim the mystery of the gospel "with boldness" (Eph. 6:19) and with the anointing of the Holy Spirit (I Cor. 2:4-5).**
- **that the Holy Spirit will open the minds and hearts of those who hear the preaching of the Church, that they may believe and be saved (Mk. 16:16; Acts 11:14).**
- **that the Pope will be empowered by the Holy Spirit to carry out his special role as successor to St. Peter and so will be a solid rock of faith on which the Church can be built up in the Holy Spirit (Mt. 16:13-20; Lk. 22:32; Acts 9:31).**
- **that all Christians will be zealous to share their faith in Jesus with others and will be empowered by the gifts and charisms of the Holy Spirit (Acts 11:19-21).**

- that the Holy Spirit will accompany the preaching of the gospel with signs and wonders (Mk. 16:17-20; Acts 5:12; I Cor. 2:4-5).
- for all missionaries that they will be empowered by the Holy Spirit to bring the Kingdom of God to all peoples.
- that the Kingdom of God will be proclaimed and believed, especially in the country of _____.
- for the conversion of all non-Christians to true faith in Jesus Christ, especially for _____.
- for those who have fallen away from their faith in Christ, that the gift of faith will be restored to them. We pray especially for _____.
- for all who have never heard the gospel, that preachers will be sent to them and that they will open their hearts to hear and believe.
- for those whose minds have been blinded by "the god of this age" (II Cor. 4:4) that God will deliver them from the spirit of unbelief.

Jesus taught his disciples the mysteries of the Kingdom of God. (Mt. 5:1-2ff.) He also commissioned his Church to teach "all nations" (Mt. 28:16-20). And so we pray

- that the Church and its teachers will teach the pure and complete gospel without error or omission.
- for teachers of religious education, for those who teach in our seminaries, universities, and colleges, and for teachers in our grade schools, middle schools, and high schools.
- that parents will be anointed to teach the gospel to their children—especially to lead them to a personal knowledge and love of Jesus.

Jesus proclaimed the Kingdom of God through the forgiveness of sins. He also commissioned his Church to continue this ministry (Lk. 24:47; John 20:22-23; James 5:15-16). And so we pray

- that the Church will faithfully carry out its ministry to bring God's mercy and forgiveness to all people.
- that the Church will clearly proclaim both the mercy of God and the reality of sin—so that through the Church, the Holy Spirit will "convict the world of sin" (John 16:8) and bring it to repentance.
- that the Church will clearly announce to the world God's call to repentance (II Cor. 5:20) and reconciliation (Mt. 5:23-26).
- for a renewed appreciation of the Sacrament of Reconciliation and its more frequent use by the faithful.
- for the grace of conversion for ourselves and for others (especially for _____).

Jesus proclaimed and established the Kingdom of God by healing the sick (Mt. 4:24). He likewise commissioned his disciples to heal the sick (Mt. 10:8) and thus continue his own healing ministry. And so we pray
- that through the power of the Holy Spirit the ministry of healing will flourish more fully in the life of the Church.
- that Jesus would heal _____ .

Jesus raised people from the dead (Mt. 11:5; Lk. 7:11-17; 8:49-56; John 11:38-44) and commanded his disciples to do likewise (Mt. 10:8; Acts 9:40-41; 20:7-12). And so we pray
- that God would endow the Church with supernatural faith to raise the dead when this is in accord with God's will and the clear prompting of the Holy Spirit.

The first recorded work of Jesus in the gospel of Mark was to deliver a man from an unclean spirit. (Mark 1:21-28) The apostle John tells us that "the Son of God was revealed to destroy the works of the devil" (I John 3:8). And Paul too reminds us that the Father has "delivered us from the power of darkness and transferred us to the kingdom of his beloved Son" (Col 1:13). Jesus commissioned his Church to continue his ministry of deliverance. And so through this mystery of the rosary we pray

- that Jesus' ministry of deliverance from evil spirits will be renewed in the Church.
- that all who need deliverance will find ready help through the Church's ministry of deliverance.

Petitions Based on the Lord's Prayer

Jesus gave his disciples the prayer of the Kingdom of God when he gave them the "Our Father." And so we make the petitions of the Lord's Prayer our own as we pray

- that all people will come to know God as their loving Father through the proclamation of the Gospel (Is. 63:16; Mal. 2:10; Mt. 11:27; Rom. 8:15-16; Gal. 4:6).
- that the Father's Name will be held in honor and spoken with reverence by all people (Ex. 20:7; Mal. 1:6,11).
- that the Kingdom of God will reign in the hearts and minds of all people.
- that God's will might be done in our lives as fully and perfectly as it is done by the angels and saints in heaven.
- that all people will be given both the spiritual and the physical bread they need to foster God's life in them.
- that God would put in our hearts the grace to forgive others so that we too may receive God's forgiveness.
- that God will strengthen all people in temptation and keep them from falling into sin (I Cor. 10:13; Jude 24-25).
- that God will deliver the whole world from the power of the evil one (Rev. 20:1-3,10).

As an act of faith you may conclude this decade of the rosary by praying:

We thank you, Father, for giving us the grace we have asked for through this holy mystery.

You may wish to add your own intentions below.

THE TRANSFIGURATION OF JESUS

Matthew 17:1-8; Mark 9:2-8, Luke 9:28-36; II Peter 1:16-18.

The mystery of the Transfiguration can be understood only in the light of Jesus' predictions of his sufferings, death, and resurrection and at the heart of his journey to Jerusalem to suffer and die for us in obedience to the will of the Father. In the Transfiguration the Father testifies to his Son and to his Son's way of obedience by glorifying him in the presence of Moses and Elijah and Peter, James, and John. The Father strengthens Jesus for the journey to the cross by giving him an experience of his glory and by affirming him again as his beloved Son. "For the sake of the joy that lay before him he endured the cross, despising its shame" (Heb. 12:2).

Through the Transfiguration of his Son, God the Father shows us that the way of the cross is the true pathway to glory. And so we pray
- that we will follow Jesus on his way of the cross and so come to share in his glory (Rom. 8:17).
- that the Father will strengthen us to be faithful to Jesus even in darkness and suffering.
- that we will not lose heart in our trials but that our eyes will behold the glory that is to come "until the day dawns and the morning star rises in our hearts" (II Pt. 1:19).

We pray in particular
- for those who are discouraged, depressed, or in despair, that they will be strengthened by the assurance of the glory that is to come. (We pray especially for _____.)

Through this mystery we pray
- **that the Jewish people will hear the witness of Moses and Elijah testifying that Jesus is indeed the eternal Son of God.**

In the Transfiguration of Jesus the Apostles experienced the "glory of God on the face of Jesus Christ" (II Cor. 4:6). And so we pray
- **for the gift of contemplation, that "all of us, gazing with unveiled face on the glory of the Lord," might be "transformed into the same image from glory to glory, as from the Lord who is the Spirit" (II Cor. 3:18).**
- **that graces of mystical prayer will be poured out upon all Christians.**

God has destined us to share the glory of his Son (Rom. 8:30; Col. 3:4; II Pt. 1:4). And so we pray
- **that the Church will be transfigured in the glory of Jesus and so become his bride "without spot or wrinkle" and "holy and without blemish" in his sight (Eph. 5:37).**
- **That the whole world will be transfigured by the glory of Jesus (Rom. 8:18-21; Is. 6:3).**

God the Father testifies that Jesus is his "beloved Son" and tells us to "listen to him" (Mt. 17:5). And so we pray
- **that we will hear the voice of the Father testifying to His Son, Jesus.**
- **that we will hear the voice of the Father affirming us as His beloved sons and daughters, so that we will not doubt His love for us even in the midst of pain and darkness.**
- **that we will always listen to Jesus and obey the word that he speaks to us.**

As an act of faith you may conclude this decade of the rosary by praying:
We thank you, Father, for giving us the grace we have asked for through this holy mystery.

You may wish to add your own intentions below.

THE INSTITUTION
OF THE HOLY EUCHARIST

Matthew 26:17-30; Mark 14:12-26; Luke 22:7-20; I Corinthians 11:23-34.

In this mystery we celebrate Jesus' self-giving, sacrificial love. "Christ loved us and handed himself over for us as a sacrificial offering to God" (Eph. 5:2). In the Eucharist, Jesus invites us to join him in his way of love and in his sacrificial offering to God. As he gives us his own Body and Blood he invites us to enter into a New Covenant with him and thus to "pass over" with him from death to eternal life.

When we celebrate the Eucharist we enter into the paschal mystery[26] of Jesus' death and resurrection. The once-and-for-all sacrifice of Jesus on the cross (Rom. 6:9-10) is made present when, through the Sacrament, we "proclaim the death of the Lord until he comes" (I Cor. 11:26). Jesus continues to be the Lamb that was slain (Rev. 5:6). His risen body still shows forth the wounds of his passion (John 20:20,27). And so we pray

- **that in each celebration of the Eucharist we might "pass over" with Jesus from death to eternal life.**
- **that the power of Jesus' death and resurrection will be released in the celebration of the Eucharist for the salvation of the world (especially for the salvation of _____).**

---

26   The word "paschal" comes from the Greek word "pescha," meaning the Feast of Passover. The ancient Passover celebrated how God saved his people from their slavery in Egypt, empowering them to "pass over" from slavery to freedom. Jesus fulfilled this salvation when he destroyed sin on the cross and enabled us to "pass over" to the eternal life of his resurrection.

86

- that through the Holy Eucharist we might "come to share in the divinity of Christ, who humbled himself to share in our humanity."[27]

We pray
- in thanksgiving for the great gift of Jesus' Body and Blood in the Eucharist.

We pray for a renewal of worship as Christians celebrate the Holy Eucharist in memory of Jesus. In particular we pray
- that Christians will worship God with hearts full of love, so that the Lord will not say of us, "This people honors me with their lips, but their hearts are far from me" (Mt. 15:8).
- that in the Eucharist Christians will be filled with the spirit of heartfelt praise.
- that Christians will realize that the Eucharist is their covenant commitment to Jesus in his Blood and that they will renew this covenant with Jesus each time they receive his Body and Blood.
- that in the celebration of the Eucharist Christians will experience the power of God, bringing them salvation, healing, and deliverance.
- that in the celebration of the Eucharist Christians will experience a foretaste of the joys of the heavenly Jerusalem in loving communion with Jesus and with the angels and saints. (See Hebrews 12:22-24.)
- that through the Eucharist all people will become one in the one Body of Christ.
- that in each celebration of the Eucharist Christians will offer themselves to God with Jesus as a "living sacrifice" (Rom. 12:1).

---

27   This prayer is said quietly by the priest at the preparation of the wine during the Offertory of the Mass.

- that through the celebration of the Eucharist Christians will learn to give their lives in sacrificial love for all people.
- that adoration of the Blessed Sacrament might take place in all the churches of the world.

Jesus in the Blessed Sacrament deserves our greatest love and respect. And so we pray
- that all who receive the Blessed Sacrament would do so with great faith and love.
- that all Christians would come to believe in the Real Presence of Jesus in the Eucharist.
- that priests and the faithful will celebrate the Eucharist with deep love and devotion.
- that God would prevent all attempts of Satanists and others to desecrate the Blessed Sacrament.
- that the Holy Spirit would draw Christians to pray in the presence of Jesus in the Blessed Sacrament.
- in atonement and reparation[28] for all sins committed against the Blessed Sacrament (especially[29] _____).

In this mystery we also recall the institution of the priesthood. And so we pray
- for all who have a share in the Sacrament of Holy Orders—for our Holy Father, the Pope, for bishops, priests, and deacons, and especially for the bishop(s), the priests and the deacons of this diocese. We pray
   - that they be filled with the spirit of holiness.

28   All sin dishonors God and therefore requires that we make atonement for that dishonor and repair the injury. Jesus made atonement to the Father for all of our sins. "He is the atoning sacrifice for our sins, and not for ours only but also for the sins of the whole world" (I John 2:2)[NRSV]. But Jesus also invites us to make atonement with him by offering his perfect sacrifice to the Father and by joining our love, prayers, and sufferings to his.
29   You might want to refer to the previous five petitions to make atonement for their neglect.

- **that they will have a personal knowledge of and love for Jesus Christ.**
- **that they will be filled with the Holy Spirit.**
- **for a faith that is deep and orthodox, true to the teachings of the Church.**
- **for faithfulness to their promises and vows.**
- **that they will have the heart of Jesus, the Good Shepherd, for their people.**
- **for the gift of inspired preaching.**
- **for the grace of courage and perseverance.**
- **that they will receive from others the support and encouragement they need.**

At the Last Supper Jesus washed the feet of his disciples and gave us the commandment, "As I have done for you, you should also do" (John 13:15). And so we pray

- **that we will have the grace to wash each other's feet—either actually or through other works of humble service.**

At the Last Supper Jesus gave us a new commandment, "As I have loved you, so you also should love one another" (John 13:34; 15:12). And so we pray

- **for the grace to live the new commandment—to love all people as Jesus loves them.**

At the Last Supper Jesus prayed "that they may all be one, as you, Father, are in me and I in you" (John 17:21). And so we pray

- **that all who partake of the one Bread will truly become one in Christ (I Cor. 10:17) and thus restore unity to the Church.**

Through the gift of his Body in the Eucharist, Jesus heals our bodies. And so we pray

- **that through the Eucharistic Body of Jesus we may realize that our body is "for the Lord, and the Lord is for the body" (I Cor.**

6:13) **and that we might always glorify God in our body** (I Cor. 6:20).
- **that our bodies might always be temples of the Holy Spirit, free from all sin** (I Cor. 6:19).

By sharing in the one Body of Christ we all become members of Christ's body, the Church. And so we pray
- **that through our sharing in the Eucharistic Body of Christ, we might honor and reverence all the members of his body, the Church.**
- **that through our sharing in the Eucharist, the unity of the Church will be restored.** (I Cor. 10:17).

As an act of faith you may conclude this decade of the rosary by praying:
We thank you, Father, for giving us the grace we have asked for through this holy mystery.

You may wish to add your own intentions below.

CHAPTER 9

THE SORROWFUL MYSTERIES

Jesus came into this world to take upon himself our sins and our sufferings. "It was our infirmities that he bore, our sufferings that he endured" (Is. 53:4; Mt. 8:17). The sorrowful mysteries of the rosary recall five very significant sufferings that Jesus endured during the final days of his life. These are:

1. The Agony Of Jesus in the Garden
2. The Scouring of Jesus at the Pillar
3. The Crowning of Jesus with Thorns
4. Jesus Carries his Cross
5. Jesus Dies on the Cross

However, it is important to remember that the entire life of Jesus was filled with suffering. He was "a man of suffering and accustomed to infirmity" (Is. 53:3).

Mary shared deeply in all the sufferings of her Son. The prophet Simeon predicted this. He told Mary, "You yourself a sword shall pierce" (Lk. 2:35). The Church recalls Mary's sufferings by selecting seven of them, the **Seven Sorrows of Mary**. These are:

1. The prophecy of Simeon (Lk. 2:34-35)
2. The flight into Egypt (Mt. 2:13-15)
3. Losing Jesus in the temple (Lk. 2:41-52)
4. Meeting Jesus as he carried his cross
5. Standing by the cross of Jesus (John 19:25-27)
6. Receiving the body of Jesus as it is taken down from the cross
7. Jesus is laid in the tomb (John 19:38-42)

The first three of the seven sorrows I have placed with the Joyful Mysteries where they fit chronologically. The other four I have placed with the Sorrowful Mysteries.

Besides these seven sorrows I have also included other moments of sorrow and struggle in the life of Jesus and Mary that deserve mention—especially since they correspond with the sufferings of so many people today. These are:

1. The slaughter of the innocents
2. The circumcision of Jesus (when Jesus first shed his blood)
3. Letting go of Jesus when he began his public ministry
4. Surrendering Jesus to his passion
5. Seeing the heart of Jesus pierced with a lance
6. Being separated from Jesus at his ascension

I have also made mention of these sorrows where they fit chronologically.

I have also included other sufferings of Jesus that are recorded in the scriptures and which take place during his passion and death. I have mentioned them as they fit in chronologically with the five Sorrowful Mysteries. These other sufferings are:

1. Jesus' betrayal by Judas (Mt. 26:47-56; Mk. 14:43-45)
2. Jesus is arrested and put into prison (Mt. 26:47-57; Mk. 14:46-49)
3. Jesus is abandoned by his disciples (Mt. 26:56; Mk. 14:50)
4. Peter denies Jesus (Mt. 26:69-75; Mk. 14:66-72)
5. Jesus is condemned to death (Mt. 27:15-26; Mk. 15:1-15)
6. Jesus meets the women of Jerusalem

I have also included sufferings of Jesus that are commemorated in the Stations of the Cross even though these are not mentioned specifically in scripture. These are:

1. Jesus falls three times under the weight of his cross
2. Jesus meets his Mother
3. Jesus is stripped of his garments

Including these other sufferings of Jesus and Mary will help us see that all our sufferings, from childhood to old age, find an echo in the life and sufferings of Jesus and his Mother and are thus joined to theirs.

THE AGONY OF JESUS
IN THE GARDEN

Matthew 26:36-46; Mark 14:32-42; Luke 22:39-46; Hebrews 5:7-10.

In the Garden of Gethsemane Jesus reversed the sin committed in the Garden of Eden by our first parents. In loving obedience to the Father's will, Jesus accepted to suffer and die for the salvation of the world. In doing so, he reversed the disobedience of Adam and Eve, as well as our own disobedience. And so, in this decade of the rosary, we pray

- **for a wholehearted and loving acceptance of the Father's will for our lives—even when this involves sacrifice and suffering. We offer the Father the perfect obedience of Jesus in atonement for our own disobedience.**
- **for those who are facing difficult decisions or facing suffering or death—that Jesus will give them the strength to know and accept God's will for their lives in loving obedience.**

In the Garden of Gethsemane Jesus faced the mystery of pain and suffering in the world. He asked the Father that if it would be possible he would not have to experience suffering and death. And yet he surrendered to the will of his Father. Many people, faced with the suffering, pain, and evil in the world, lose faith in God. In the Garden, Jesus obtained for us the grace to go through the sufferings of this life while trusting in the Father's love for us and for all his creatures. And so through this mystery we pray

- **for those who are tempted to lose faith in God when faced with the mystery of evil, that they might trust in the Father's love for them and "hand their souls over to a faithful creator" (I Pt. 4:19).**

Mary surrendered her Son to the will of the Father and encouraged her Son to undergo his passion and death. And so we pray

- **that we will have the courage to surrender our loved ones to the will of God and encourage them to make the sacrifices they need to make.**

Jesus agonized in the garden for the salvation of every human being. He intercedes with the Father for their salvation. And so

- **we offer to the Father the agonizing prayer of Jesus for the salvation of every human being—in particular for (_____). We pray that they will have the grace of final conversion.**

In his agony in the garden Jesus took upon himself all the agonies and sufferings of every human being. And so we pray

- **that through the agonies of Jesus in the garden, the agonies and sufferings of all people will lead them to eternal life.**

Jesus tells us, "watch and pray that you may not undergo the test" (Mt. 26:41). And so we pray

- **for the strength to "watch and pray" with Jesus, even when this requires sacrifice on our part.**
- **that through Jesus' prayer in the garden we will be strengthened to overcome the weakness of our flesh (Mt. 26:41) and be faithful to prayer each day.**

Jesus was betrayed in the garden by Judas (Mt. 26:47-56; etc.). And so we pray

- **for the strength to love and forgive those who betray us and for others who are experiencing betrayal in their lives.**

In his sufferings Jesus was abandoned by his disciples. They could not watch one hour with him. And when Jesus was arrested "all the disciples left him and fled" (Mt. 26:56).

And so we pray
- **for all who have been abandoned by their loved ones or by those they trusted, that they might draw strength from Jesus' abiding presence and receive from others the help they need.**

Jesus refused to use violence to defend himself. And so we pray
- **for the grace to love and forgive our enemies and to "overcome evil by good" (Rom. 12:21). We pray for this same grace for others and for the nations of the world.**

Jesus was arrested in the garden and led off to prison. And so we pray
- **for all who are in prison that they might experience the saving love of Jesus and experience true inner freedom.**

Jesus was falsely accused and was condemned to death by the authorities (Mt. 26:57-68; 27:1-26; etc.). And so we pray
- **for all who have been falsely accused and unjustly condemned, that they might draw strength from the sufferings of Jesus and be vindicated by the truth (Is. 45:25).**

Despite his good intentions (Mk. 14:27-31; etc.), Peter denied that he knew Jesus (Mk. 14:66-72; etc.). And so we pray
- **for God's forgiveness for the times we have denied Jesus, especially through fear of others. We pray for the grace never to be ashamed of being Jesus' followers (Acts 4:8-22; Rom. 1:16a).**

Beginning with his Agony in the Garden and throughout his passion, Jesus suffered severe and constant pain. And so we pray
- **for all who are suffering severe or chronic pain, that their pains will be joined to the pains of Jesus and that they might receive the relief and comfort they need.**
- **that we would willingly bear our sufferings with Jesus in the sure hope that they are "producing for us an eternal weight of glory beyond all comparison" (II Cor. 4:17).**

As an act of faith you may conclude this decade of the rosary by praying:
We thank you, Father, for giving us the grace we have asked for through this holy mystery.

You may wish to add your own intentions below.

THE SCOURGING OF JESUS AT THE PILLAR

Matthew 27:26; Mark 15:15; Luke 23:22; John 19:1; I Peter 2:24b; Isaiah 53:5.

Scourging was a part of crucifixion. For Roman citizens only, scourging was limited to 39 blows. (See II Corinthians 11:24.) Not being a Roman citizen, Jesus could be beaten at the whim of his executioners.

Isaiah prophesied of Jesus that "he was pierced for our offenses, crushed for our sins. Upon him was the chastisement that makes us whole. By his stripes we were healed" (Is. 53:5). And so we pray
- **that by Jesus' scourging at the pillar we might be healed of every affliction of body, soul, and spirit. We pray especially for the healing of _____.**

Since the sufferings of Jesus were endured because of our sins, we have reason to know that he endured specific sufferings to atone for specific sins. We might suppose that Jesus endured the sufferings of the scourging to atone for our sins of the flesh. We would do well then to offer these sufferings of Jesus to the Father
- **in atonement for our sins of the flesh and for the grace to overcome these sins—that by his stripes we may be healed (Is. 53:5).**
- **in atonement for sins of illicit sex, for over-indulgence in eating and drinking, for sins of vanity (I Pt. 3:3-5), the misuse of drugs and alcohol, and for all forms excessive self-indulgence. We pray for the grace to overcome these sins through the merits of Jesus' scourging.**

In Jesus' scourging we see how sin disfigures us. And so we pray

- **that through Jesus' scourging at the pillar we may be restored to the "image and likeness of God" to be "without blemish" in his sight** (Eph. 5:27).

By his scourging Jesus brings healing to all who are abused by others. And so we pray

- **for children who are abused physically, emotionally, or sexually and who lose their innocence through the evil influence of others.**
- **for victims of violence in homes, especially women and children.**
- **for those who are sexually exploited through rape or pornography.**
- **for Christians who are persecuted for their faith, that they may be strengthened by the sufferings of Jesus.**
- **for victims of ritual abuse or other forms of misguided religious zeal.**

Jesus was unjustly condemned and tortured. We pray

- **for all who have been unjustly condemned, put in prison, tortured, or put to death—that God's mercy will sustain them and God's justice restore to them all they have lost.**

When others hurt us or our loved ones, we are often tempted to hate our abusers, to retaliate against them, to want to "get even," to curse them or cause them injury. St. Peter tells us of Jesus that "when he was insulted, he returned no insult; when he suffered, he did not threaten; instead, he handed himself over to the one who judges justly" (I Pt. 2:23). And Jesus himself taught us: "Love your enemies, do good to those who hate you, bless those who curse you, pray for those who mistreat you" (Lk. 6:27-28).[30] And so through Jesus' scourging we pray

---

30   See also I Peter 3:9 and Romans 12:17-21.

- for the grace to forgive our abusers, to pray for them and to bless them. We pray for this grace especially for (_____) and for the peoples and nations that especially need this grace (_____).

As an act of faith you may conclude this decade of the rosary by praying:
We thank you, Father, for giving us the grace we have asked for through this holy mystery.

You may wish to add your own intentions below.

THE CROWNING OF JESUS WITH THORNS

Matthew 27:27-31; Mark 15:16-20; John 19:2-3.

The crowning with thorns was a mockery of Jesus' claim to be king. The mockery included not only the crown of thorns, but also stripping off his clothes, putting on him a scarlet cloak, putting a reed in his right hand (as his scepter), kneeling before him and saying "Hail, King of the Jews!," spitting on him and striking his head with a reed.

In this decade of the rosary, we offer these sufferings of Jesus

- **in atonement for our sins of seeking prestige, status, recognition and honor from others, and for the pride that goes with titles.**
- **in atonement for the sins that go with the misuse of power and authority: controlling and using others, lording it over them, seeking to be served by others, desiring favors and special treatment.**
- **in atonement for the sins of those who seek higher positions in government and in the church—for prideful ambition, lies, deceit, cheating, buying favors, offering bribes, making payoffs, and slandering others in order to advance oneself.**

We pray

- **for the grace to follow the example of Jesus' humility by serving others and not seeking our own glory, but only the glory of God and the salvation of souls.**

We pray
- for those in positions of authority in local, state, national, and world governments, that they will serve in obedience to the laws of God and in the spirit of generosity, justice, and love for all people.

We pray
- for parents, that they will exercise authority over their children with wisdom, love, fairness, and humility.

We pray
- for those who exercise authority in business and finance, that they will exercise their authority as stewards of God's resources in obedience to God and in the spirit of justice, generosity and humility.

After Jesus was crowned with thorns, Pilate led him out to show him to the people and said, "Behold, the man!" (John 19:5). "There was in him no stately bearing to make us look at him, nor appearance that would attract us to him" (Is. 53:2). And yet Jesus shows us what it means to be truly human. He is "the image of the invisible God" (Col. 1:15) and by his sufferings he refashions us so that we too can once again bear the image of God (Gen. 1:26-27). And so we pray
- that we will learn from Jesus what it means to be truly human and that we will be recreated in him (Eph. 2:10; 4:24) in the image and likeness of God.
- in reparation for sins of vanity regarding appearance in body or in clothing.

Through his crowning with thorns, Jesus also atones for sins of the mind. From the time of Adam and Eve, we have chosen to believe the lies of Satan. We often eat from the Tree of the Knowledge of Good and Evil instead of eating from the Tree of Life—the tree of God's wisdom. (See Proverbs 3:18.) We have "exchanged the truth of God for a lie" (Rom. 1:25). Our thoughts have become "corrupted from a sincere and pure commitment to Christ" (II Cor. 11:3). Through his crowning with thorns Jesus gives us the grace to "take every thought captive in obedience to Christ" (II Cor. 10:54). When our minds are bombarded by evil thoughts, Jesus' crown of thorns becomes our "helmet of salvation" (Eph. 6:17), our "helmet on the day of battle" (Ps. 140:8). And so though this mystery we pray

- **that Jesus' crown of thorns will purify our minds from all evil thoughts and from all the lies of the evil one and fill our minds with the light and truth of the Holy Spirit** (Phil. 4:8).
- **that Jesus' crown of thorns will help us truly put on "the mind of Christ"** (I Cor. 2:16).
- **that Jesus' crown of thorns will protect the minds of our children and youth from the deceptions of false teachers and from the false values of our society** (I Cor. 3:18-20; I Tim. 1:3-7; 6:3-5; II Tim. 4:1-5).
- **that through Jesus' crowning with thorns, the leaders of countries will think thoughts of peace and not of war** (Is. 2:2-5; Ps. 120:6-7).

As an act of faith you may conclude this decade of the rosary by praying:
We thank you, Father, for giving us the grace we have asked for through this holy mystery.

You may wish to add your own intentions below.

JESUS CARRIES HIS CROSS

Matthew 27:32; Mark 15:21; Luke 23:26-31; John 19:17.

Jesus told his disciples, "Whoever wishes to come after me must deny himself, take up his cross, and follow me" (Mt. 16:24). Jesus embraced his cross as the instrument for the salvation of the world. His love for his Father and his love for souls urged him on.

And so in this decade of the rosary we pray
- **that the love of Christ would impel us** (II Cor. 5:14) **to carry our crosses together with Jesus.**

After having been scourged and crowned with thorns, Jesus was led away to be crucified. And so we pray
- **for all who have received a sentence of death that they will surrender their lives to Jesus who died for them that they might have eternal life.**

The way of the cross was painful and exhausting, but Jesus persevered. Jesus could have said, "I have suffered enough," and gone no further. But instead, he pressed on to the end, refusing to count the cost, determined to drink the cup of suffering to the last drop. And so he gained for us the grace to persevere in carrying our crosses. In this decade of the rosary, therefore, we pray
- **for the grace of perseverance for those who are tempted to give up, to abandon their faith, or to commit suicide.**

In carrying his cross Jesus showed himself to be the Good Shepherd who kept looking for his lost sheep—expending the last ounce of his energy until he found the sheep that was lost. We pray

- **that we will have the zeal of Jesus for lost souls.**
- **that every member of the church, especially parents and those entrusted with the care of souls (bishops, priests, and deacons), will have the zeal of Jesus for souls and will spare no effort for their salvation.**

Simon the Cyrenian helped Jesus carry his cross. We too are called to help others carry their crosses. "Bear one another's burdens, and so you will fulfill the law of Christ" (Gal. 6:2). And so we pray
- **for the grace to have compassion for the sufferings of others and to help them carry their crosses.**

Even in his own sufferings Jesus took time to console the women of Jerusalem. And so we pray
- **for the grace to move beyond our own problems, concerns, and sufferings and to reach out to others who are suffering or in need.**

Jesus fell three times under the weight of the cross. We too often fall under the weight of our burdens and sometimes even fall into sin. And so we pray
- **that we will know that when we fall, Jesus is always with us and is ready to lift us up and forgive us.**

While carrying his cross Jesus met his Mother. Mary encouraged her Son, and her Son encouraged her. And so we pray
- **that Mary would help us see Jesus in all who are suffering and teach us how to comfort them.**[31]

Tradition tells us that Veronica wiped the face of Jesus. Jesus left the imprint of his face on the veil. He also leaves his imprint on everyone who does an act of kindness in his name and will one day say to them,

---

31   This petition is based on one of the seven sorrows of Mary.

"Come, you who are blessed by my Father. Inherit the kingdom prepared for you from the foundation of the world" (Mt. 25:34). And so we pray

- **for the grace to reach out like Veronica and give comfort to all who are suffering.**

As an act of faith you may conclude this decade of the rosary by praying:
We thank you, Father, for giving us the grace we have asked for through this holy mystery.

You may wish to add your own intentions below.

JESUS DIES ON THE CROSS

Matthew 27:33-56; Mark 15:22-41; Luke 23:33-49; John 19:18-37.

On the cross Jesus made the supreme sacrifice of himself to the Father. He took upon himself all the evils of the world: all sin, suffering, sickness, and death itself. He took on himself all the evils perpetrated in the world by Satan and thereby destroyed all the works of Satan and freed the world from Satan's grasp. Jesus destroyed the kingdom of Satan and established the Kingdom of God. "Indeed the Son of God was revealed to destroy the works of the devil" (I John 3:8b). Paul tells us that if the "rulers of this age" (Satan and the evil spirits) had known that this would happen, "they would not have crucified the Lord of glory" (I Cor. 2:8). And so we pray

- **that by the cross of Jesus the whole world will be saved and set free from the power of sin and evil.**
- **that by the Blood of Jesus all the powers of darkness throughout the world will be destroyed, especially as these operate through Satanism, witchcraft, and other occult practices.**
- **that the power of the cross will remove the spiritual blindness that prevents people from believing in Jesus (II Cor. 4:3-4).**

Through his death on the cross, Jesus reconciled us to God (Rom. 5:10; Col. 1:20; II Cor. 5:17-18). And so

- **we thank Jesus for reconciling us to the Father and ask him to lead us to an ever more loving intimacy with the Father (Mt. 11:27; John 1:18; Eph. 2:18; 3:12).**

Through his death Jesus has reconciled us to one another, "making peace by the blood of his cross" (Col. 1:20) and breaking down "the dividing wall of enmity" (Eph. 2:14). And so we pray

- **that the power of the Blood of Jesus will heal the wounds of division and hostility among peoples, nations, races, religions, churches, and members of families (especially between _____ and _____).**

On the cross Jesus atoned for all our sins and washed them away in his precious Blood. And so in this mystery of the rosary

- **we offer to the Father the Blood of Jesus in atonement for our sins, for the sins of our loved ones, and for the sins of the whole world.**

we pray also

- **that through faith and repentance all people will receive the forgiveness of their sins, offered to them by Jesus (especially _____).**

Jesus died for us so that our death would lead to eternal life with God. And so we pray

- **for all who are dying, that through the death of Jesus, they will be saved and enter eternal life with God in heaven. (We pray especially for _____.)**

Through his death on the cross Jesus has given us access to God (Eph. 2:6,18; 3:12). Heaven was opened. The veil of the temple, separating us from the Holy of Holies, was torn in two (Mt. 27:51). Through his Blood we have gained entrance into the heavenly sanctuary (Heb. 9:11-12; 10:19-20). And so in this mystery

- **we ask Jesus to bring us by faith into the Holy of Holies to worship God the Father together with him.**

By the Blood of Jesus we are cleansed, saved, and protected from the evil one. In this mystery

- **we ask Jesus to cleanse us more and more from our sins and to cleanse those for whom we pray** (Rev. 7:14; Ps. 51:4).
- **we ask Jesus to save us and to save those for whom we pray (especially _____).**
- **we pray that the power of Jesus' cross and his shed Blood will destroy the work of the evil one in ourselves and in those for whom we pray (especially _____).**
- **we pray that the Blood of Jesus will cover us, cover our loved ones and all for whom we are praying (especially _____)—and protect them from all evil** (Ex. 12:23).

Through our faith and our baptism into Jesus' death and resurrection we have died with Christ to our old self, which was under the power of sin and Satan, and we now live for God in Christ Jesus (Romans 6:1-18). In this mystery we pray

- **that our old self, with its "passions and desires," will be crucified with Christ and that we will become a new creation in him** (Gal. 5:24; 6:15; Eph. 4:24; II Cor. 5:17).
- **that by sharing in the sufferings of Jesus and being "conformed to his death," we may also share in his resurrection** (Phil. 3:10-11).
- **that by being "crucified with Christ," it will no longer be we who live, but Christ who lives in us** (Gal. 2:19-20).

Through his death Jesus left us our full inheritance—all that he had received from his Father. "Where there is a will, the death of the testator must be established. For a will takes effect only at death; it has no force while the testator is alive" (Heb. 9:16-17). And so we pray

- **that through the death of Jesus we might receive our full inheritance as sons and daughters of God.**

On the cross Jesus loved us "to the end"[32] (John 13:1) and fulfilled his own words that "no one has greater love than this, to lay down one's life for one's friends" (John 15:13). And so we pray

- **that we would know how much Jesus loves us and in turn grow in our love for Jesus crucified.**

At his crucifixion Jesus was stripped of his garments. By suffering in this way, Jesus made atonement for sins of immodesty, indecent dress, rape, and the misuse of the body. And so we pray

- **in atonement for sins of immodesty, indecent dress, rape, and other sins of impurity.**

Jesus was nailed to the cross. By this suffering Jesus made atonement for the sins we commit with our hands, such as hurting others, stealing, and improper touching. He also made atonement for sins in which our feet take us to places of sin. And so we pray

- **in atonement for sins that we and others commit with our hands and feet.**

By being nailed to the cross Jesus surrendered his freedom in order to set us free. And so we pray

- **that by being nailed to the cross, Jesus would set us free to serve God (Lk. 1:74) and to serve one another through love (Gal. 5:13).**

Mary stood by the Cross of Jesus. She was the model of a faithful disciple. She would not abandon her Son in his bitter sufferings and death.[33] And so we pray

- **that like Mary we will always be faithful to Jesus even in the midst of suffering and persecution.**

---

32   The expression "to the end" probably has a double meaning of "to the end of his life on earth" and "without limit, to the fullest possible extent."

33   The following two petitions are based on one of the seven sorrows of Mary.

I 1 2

- for those who have been abandoned by family and friends, that they will experience the faithful and loving presence of Jesus and Mary and the consolation of the Holy Spirit.

Mary, together with her Son, forgave those who crucified him. And so we pray
- **that, through the intercession of Mary, parents will have the grace to forgive those who have hurt or killed their children.**

Mary surrendered her Son to the Father's will and so offered him for the salvation of the world. In doing so, she exercised her priesthood, showing all Christians how to exercise the priesthood of all believers (I Pt. 2:5; Rev. 1:6). And so
- **together with Mary we offer Jesus to the Father for the salvation of the world (especially for the salvation of _____).**

Mary had to witness all the sufferings of her Son as he was stripped of his garments, nailed to the cross, suffered the agony of the cross, and bore the taunts of those who hated him. She suffered also after his death as he was pierced with a lance, taken down from the cross, laid in her arms, and buried.[34] And so we pray
- **that, through the sufferings of Mary, mothers and fathers will be comforted in the sufferings and in the death of their children.**

The Seven Last Words of Jesus

(1) On the cross Jesus gave us to his mother, "Woman, behold your son," and he gave his mother to us, "Behold, your mother" (John 19:27). And so we pray

---

34   This petition is based on the last three of the seven sorrows of Mary. See pages 91-92.

- **that we might come to know Mary as our mother and experience her motherly care in our lives. We pray this especially for _____.**

(2) On the cross Jesus experienced the absence of his Father, "My God, my God, why have you forsaken me?" (Mt. 27:46) And so we pray

- **for all those who feel abandoned by God, that through the abandonment of Jesus they might come to believe and experience God's love for them. (We pray especially for _____.)**

(3) On the cross Jesus forgave those who crucified him, "Father, forgive them, they know not what they do" (Lk. 23:34). Mary also forgave those who crucified her Son. And so we pray

- **for the grace to forgive those who have hurt us and those who have hurt the ones we love.**

(4) Jesus offered eternal life to the criminal on the cross who repented (Lk. 23:40-43), and so we pray

- **for the grace of final repentance for all who have led lives of sin, especially for those who are near death.**

(5) On the cross Jesus said, "I thirst" (John 19:28). Jesus thirsted and continues to thirst for the salvation of souls. And so we pray

- **that we might thirst for the salvation of souls as Jesus did, and satisfy Jesus' thirst by bringing souls to him.**

(6) On the cross Jesus finished the work the Father had given him to do (John 17:4), and so he could say: "It is finished" (John 19:30). We pray

- **that we will faithfully accomplish all that the Father has given us to do during the course of our lives.**

(7) At the moment of his death Jesus trusted in his Father, "Father, into your hands I commend my spirit" (Lk. 23:46). And so we pray
- **for those who are dying that they will not despair but will trust in God's mercy offered them by Jesus.**
- **that all who are dying will "die in the Lord" (Rev. 14:13), believing in him and loving him, and so be saved.**

After his death, Jesus' heart was pierced with the soldier's lance, and blood and water flowed out (John 19:34). His Blood symbolizes the gift of the Eucharist; the water, the gift of Baptism. Both the Blood and the Water bring us the gift of the Holy Spirit. (See John 4:14; 7:38-39; John 2:10.) We pray
- **that through Baptism and the Holy Eucharist, we will receive all the graces flowing from the Heart of Jesus.**
- **that we will draw living water with joy from "the fountain of salvation" (Is. 12:3) and drink deeply of the new wine of the Holy Spirit (John 2:10; Mt. 9:17; Acts 2:13).**

After his death, Jesus was taken down from the cross and laid in the arms of his mother. A sorrow so deep filled her heart, a sorrow shared by so many mothers and fathers as they suffer the death of their children and other loved ones.[35] And so we pray
- **that through the sufferings of Mary, all those who mourn the death of their loved ones, especially mothers and fathers, will be comforted and find hope in the assurance of the resurrection.**

Mary fulfilled the beatitude, "Blessed are they who mourn, for they will be comforted" (Mt. 5:4). Mary mourns for her Son; she also mourns for us and for all who wander far from God. And so we pray
- **that through the tears of Mary all souls will be brought back to God, (especially _____).**

---

35   This petition and the next two petitions are also related to the seven sorrows of Mary—listed on pages 91-92.

The body of Jesus was buried in the tomb (Mt. 27:57-61)—a scene so often repeated in the history of the world. Jesus shared fully in our death. He took upon himself the sentence of death pronounced over Adam (Gen. 2:17; 3:3,19). But he was destined to overcome death by the power of his resurrection. And so we pray

- **that by sharing in the death and burial of Jesus, we might rise with him to eternal life** (Rom. 6:5-11; John 5:28-29).

After his death on the cross Jesus "went to preach to the spirits in prison, who had once been disobedient" (I Pt. 3:19-20). He brought them his atoning Blood and the full remission of their sins. And so we pray

- **for the souls in Purgatory, that Jesus will grant them the full remission of their sins through his atoning Blood.**
- **for the healing of our ancestors, for the forgiveness of their sins and for their entrance into eternal life (and especially for the soul(s) of _____).**

As an act of faith you may conclude this decade of the rosary by praying:
We thank you, Father, for giving us the grace we have asked for through this holy mystery.

You may wish to add your own intentions below.

CHAPTER 10

THE GLORIOUS MYSTERIES

The Glorious Mysteries of the rosary bring God's saving work to completion. These mysteries are:

1. The Resurrection of Jesus from the Dead
2. The Ascension of Jesus into Heaven
3. The Gift of the Holy Spirit on Pentecost
4. The Assumption of Mary into Heaven
5. The Crowning of Mary as Queen

In the Glorious Mysteries we celebrate the marvelous reality that God has restored his glory to us. In doing so, he reverses the fallen, sinful condition of our human nature that we inherited from Adam. St. Paul describes this condition when he says, "All have sinned and are deprived of the glory of God" (Rom. 3:23). This echoes the sad cry of the wife of Phinehas, "Gone is the glory from Israel" (I Sam. 4:21-22). (See also Ezekiel 10:18-23.) Now, in Jesus, the glory of God is given back to us! "Those he justified, he also glorified" (Rom. 8:30).

In fact God's glory is being restored to ALL of creation. As Paul says, creation itself will "be set free from slavery to corruption and share in the glorious freedom of the children of God" (Rom. 8:21). This is what we celebrate in the Glorious Mysteries of the rosary.

In the first two mysteries—Jesus' resurrection and ascension—we see fulfillment of this mystery in the person of Jesus himself. His human nature is glorified by the Father and returns in glory to the Father in heaven. In his own person he has achieved "eternal redemption." (See Hebrews 9:12.) In the last three mysteries we celebrate how the glory of this "eternal redemption" is being shared with us and with all creation.

In the third Glorious Mystery, the mystery of Pentecost, we celebrate how "all of us, gazing with unveiled face on the glory of the Lord, are being transformed into the same image from glory to glory, as from the Lord who is the Spirit" (II Cor. 3:18).

In the last two Glorious Mysteries we celebrate how God has brought the Church and creation to its perfection in glory in the person of Mary. We should not imagine that in these last two mysteries we have taken our focus off Jesus. On the contrary, we are precisely celebrating the saving work of Jesus, now brought to its perfection in creation. The other mysteries of the rosary would not be complete without these final two. Mary shines forth as a sign and promise of the glory that is to be ours. "A great sign appeared in the sky, a woman clothed with the sun, with the moon under her feet, and on her head a crown of twelve stars" (Rev. 12:1).

In the person of Mary, God gives us a "preview" of the glory that will be ours—when God will assume us all into heaven there to reign with him forever.

THE RESURRECTION OF JESUS FROM THE DEAD

Matthew 28:1-20; Mark 16:1-18; Luke 24:1-49; John 20-21; I Corinthians 15.

The resurrection of Jesus is God's victory over all the forces of darkness and evil. It also brings to completion (in the person of Jesus) God's eternal plan for the world. The risen Jesus is the beginning of God's new creation. Through him God will make all creation new. He will create a "new heaven and a new earth." (See Romans 8:19-23 and Revelation 21:1,5.) Even now, through the risen Jesus we have become a "new creation" (Gal. 6:15; II Cor. 5:17). We have been raised up with Christ, and our "life is hidden with Christ in God" (Col. 3:1-2). We can now say with St. Paul, "I live, no longer I, but Christ lives in me" (Gal. 2:20).

And so, in this decade of the rosary we pray
- **that the power of Jesus' resurrection will destroy all the forces of evil that threaten us or that are in any way at work in us and in those for whom we pray (_____).**
- **that we might know "the surpassing greatness of his power for us who believe, in accord with the exercise of his great might, which he worked in Christ, rising him from the dead"** (Eph. 1:19-20).
- **that we might know that we have died with Christ to our old self, that we have become a new creation in him, and that our life is now "hidden with Christ in God."**
- **that we can truly say, "I live, no longer I, but Christ lives in me"** (Gal. 2:20).

We pray
- that in Jesus we will live as "children of the light," that there will be no darkness of sin in us, but only the holiness and truth of God. (See Ephesians 5:8-14.)

We pray with St. Paul
- that the risen Jesus may dwell in our hearts through faith, that rooted and grounded in love we may have strength to comprehend with all the holy ones the breadth and length and height and depth, and to know the love of Christ that surpasses knowledge, so that we may be filled with all the fullness of God. (See Ephesians 3:17-19.)

The risen Jesus asked Peter three times if he loved him (John 21:15-19). He seeks our love as well. And so we pray
- that our hearts will overflow with love for our risen Savior.

Peter's love for Jesus was to overflow in a loving and careful shepherding of Jesus' flock. And so we pray
- that all who shepherd the flock of Jesus, will do so with great love and care.

The risen Jesus announces peace to us (Lk. 24:36; John 20:19,21; Eph. 2:14-18), peace with God through the forgiveness of our sins (Lk. 24:47; John 20:23), and peace with one another through reconciliation. Let us pray
- that we and those for whom we pray (_____), will experience peace with God and God's infinite divine mercy, especially through the Sacrament of Reconciliation.
- for the grace of reconciliation between individuals (_____ and _____), between nations (_____ and _____), and among all Christians.

The risen Jesus walks with us on our journey through life (Lk. 24:13-35). He speaks to us through the scriptures and invites us to recognize him in the breaking of the bread. And so we pray

- **that we will take time to let Jesus explain the scriptures to us and let him open our eyes to recognize him in the Holy Eucharist.**
- **that we might be constantly aware of Jesus' presence with us and in us and allow him to be the source of all our thoughts, words, and actions.**

Our human nature falls easily into doubt, as did the apostle Thomas (John 20:24-29). And so we pray

- **that the light of the risen Jesus will banish all doubts and fears from our hearts (from the hearts of ____) and give us (and ____) the assurance of having eternal life in him** (John 17:3; 20:31; I John 5:20).

One day Jesus "will change our lowly body to conform with his glorified body by the power that enables him also to bring all things into subjection to himself" (Phil. 3:21). And so we pray

- **for the faith to believe that one day our bodies will rise and be glorified like the body of the risen Jesus.**

As an act of faith you may conclude this decade of the rosary by praying:
We thank you, Father, for giving us the grace we have asked for through this holy mystery.

You may wish to add your own intentions below.

THE ASCENSION OF JESUS INTO HEAVEN

Luke 24:50-53; Acts 1:6-11; 2:33; Hebrews 1:3b; 7:25; 9:12,24; Psalm 2; 47; 110; Ezekiel 10:23; Zechariah 14:4.

In his ascension Jesus returns to the Father who sent him (John 16:5). He had finished the work the Father had given him to do (John 17:4). He had "obtained eternal redemption" (Heb. 9:12). And so as we pray this mystery
- **we thank Jesus for the "eternal redemption" he has obtained for us through everything he did for us from his conception to his ascension into heaven.**

In his ascension, Jesus "took his seat at the right hand of the Majesty on high" (Heb. 1:3). God the Father enthroned his Son at his right hand as King and Lord of the universe. And so Jesus can say, "All power in heaven and on earth has been given to me" (Mt. 28:18). And so in this mystery of the ascension
- **we acknowledge Jesus to be our Lord and King—Lord and King of our hearts, our family, our parish, our city, our country, and of our world and we believe that even now he is establishing his Kingdom (especially in our _____).**

We pray
- **that everyone in the world (especially _____) will accept Jesus as their Lord and Savior.**

It was prophesied of Jesus in his ascension, "The scepter of your sovereign might the Lord will extend from Zion. The Lord says: 'Rule over your enemies!'" (Ps. 110:2). And so in this mystery we pray

- **that Jesus would destroy all the powers of darkness at work in our world, in our nation, in our Church, and in our families (especially the evil of _____).**

We all have problems that seem to be hopeless. And yet Jesus is Lord and Master of these problems also. "Nothing will be impossible for God" (Lk. 1:37). And so

- **in this decade of the rosary we surrender all our problems to you, Lord Jesus, (especially _____). We declare you to be Lord of these problems. We put you in complete charge of them and trust you to manifest your glory through them** (John 11:40).

In his ascension, Jesus enters into the heavenly sanctuary to "appear before God on our behalf" (Heb. 9:24). In the Old Testament the high priest entered the Holy of Holies once a year on the Day of Atonement to make atonement for the sins of the people by offering the blood of bulls and goats. Now Jesus enters the true sanctuary to offer to God his own blood in atonement for the sins of the world. And so in this mystery,

- **we ask you Lord Jesus to offer your Blood to the Eternal Father in atonement for our sins and the sins of others, and we thank you for your perfect and complete atonement.**

In his ascension, Jesus goes before his heavenly Father to intercede for us. "He is always able to save those who approach God through him, since he lives forever to make intercession for them" (Heb. 7:25). In this decade of the rosary we give Jesus our prayers to offer to the Father, and we trust that Jesus' prayer will be answered. "All you ask the Father in my name he will give you" (John 15:16). And so

- **we join our prayers to yours, Lord Jesus, and trust that in your name we have received the answer to these prayers, especially (_____).**

In his ascension, Jesus receives from his Father his full inheritance. He receives ALL the promises of God, the fullness of the Holy Spirit. (See II Corinthians 1:20 and Galatians 3:14-16.) Jesus receives his full inheritance in order to give it to us. He ascended into heaven "that he might fill all things" (Eph. 4:10). "Exalted at the right hand of God, he received the promise of the Holy Spirit from the Father and poured it forth, as you both see and hear" (Acts 2:33). God has "blessed us in Christ with every spiritual blessing in the heavens" (Eph. 1:3). And so

- **in this mystery, we thank you, Lord Jesus, for obtaining for us our full inheritance and we believe that in you we now possess our inheritance. We claim especially the following grace of our inheritance (_____).**

In his ascension, Jesus tells us, "I am going to prepare a place for you" (John 14:2). And so we pray

- **that we, and especially all who are dying, will know that Jesus has prepared a place for us in heaven.**

God has already "seated us with him in the heavens in Christ Jesus" (Eph. 2:6). And so

- **we pray for the faith to accept even now our place in heaven with Jesus at the right hand of the Father and for the grace to live as citizens of heaven** (Eph. 2:19; Phil. 3:20).

After Jesus' ascension "two men dressed in white garments" announced that "this Jesus who has been taken up from you into heaven will return in the same way as you have seen him going into heaven" (Acts 1:10-11). And so we pray

- **that we will look forward to Jesus' return with great joy and peace, and not give in to idle speculation about the time of his coming or give into fear of the troubles that will precede it.**
- **that we will be prepared to receive Jesus when he comes, by living now with great faith, hope, and love of God and our neighbor.**

As an act of faith you may conclude this decade of the rosary by praying:
We thank you, Father, for giving us the grace we have asked for through this holy mystery.

You may wish to add your own intentions below.

THE GIFT OF THE HOLY SPIRIT ON PENTECOST

Acts 1:4-5, 14; 2:1-13; John 15:26-16:15; 20:22.

Jesus told his disciples to "wait for the promise of the Father" and added that in a few days they would be "baptized with the Holy Spirit" (Acts 1:4-5). In order to prepare themselves to receive the Holy Spirit they all "devoted themselves with one accord to prayer, together with some women, and Mary the mother of Jesus, and his brothers" (Acts 1:14). And so in this decade of the rosary we too enlist the prayers of Mary in order to be disposed to receive the Gift of the Holy Spirit. As Mary conceived and formed Jesus in her womb through the Holy Spirit, so also she conceives and forms the members of Christ's body through the Holy Spirit.

As we pray this decade of the rosary it is helpful to be aware of the many and varied gifts and graces of the Holy Spirit and to ask for these graces in our prayer. Some of these are mentioned here.

Jesus said, "I have come to set the earth on fire, and how I wish it were already blazing!" (Lk. 12:49) And so we pray
- **that Jesus would enkindle in us and in all people the fire of the Holy Spirit, so that our hearts will be aflame with the love of God and with zeal for God's Kingdom.**

Through the Holy Spirit the Church is born and is made "one, holy, catholic, and apostolic." And so we pray
- **that the Holy Spirit will be poured out upon the Church in a new Pentecost, and that each of us will enter more deeply into**

the mystery of the Church which is "one, holy, catholic, and apostolic."

Through the gift of the Holy Spirit we have been made sharers "in the divine nature" (II Pt. 1:4) and so are begotten as children of God (John 3:3-7; Gal. 4:4-7). And so we pray
- **that through the Holy Spirit we might share more fully in the divine nature and so live as true children of God.**

When God created Adam, he "blew into his nostrils the breath of life, and so man became a living being" (Gen. 2:7). The risen Jesus now breathes on us and says, "Receive the Holy Spirit" (John 20:22). By doing this, Jesus makes us a "new creation" (Gal. 6:15; II Cor. 5:17; Eph. 2:10). And so we pray
- **that Jesus would breathe his Holy Spirit into us and recreate us in his own image and likeness.**

The Holy Spirit reveals the Father to us. He brings us revelation that God is our loving "Abba," and that we are his children in Jesus (Gal. 4:6). And so we pray
- **that we might experience the Holy Spirit crying out in our hearts "Abba, Father" and so come to know that we are children of God.**

The Spirit reveals Jesus to us. "No one can say 'Jesus is Lord' except by the Holy Spirit" (I Cor. 12:3). And so we pray
- **that the Holy Spirit will reveal Jesus to us and give us a personal knowledge and love of him.**

The Holy Spirit is the Spirit of divine love. "The love of God has been poured out into our hearts through the Holy Spirit that has been given to us" (Rom. 5:5). And so we pray

- **that the love of God would be poured out into our hearts through the Holy Spirit and become within us a fountain overflowing to eternal life.** (See John 4:14.)

The Holy Spirit produces good fruit in us. "The fruit of the Spirit is love, joy, peace, patience, kindness, generosity, faithfulness, gentleness, self-control" (Gal. 5:22-23). As you pray this decade of the rosary, choose one of these fruits that you especially want the Holy Spirit to produce in you. And so we pray

- **that the Holy Spirit will produce in us the fruit of (_____) (love, joy, peace, patience, kindness, generosity, faithfulness, gentleness, self-control).**

The Holy Spirit produces in the church many "manifestations" in order to build up the Body of Christ. Paul lists nine special manifestations of the Spirit, "the expression of wisdom, the expression of knowledge, faith, gifts of healing, mighty deeds, prophecy, discernment of spirits, varieties of tongues, interpretation of tongues" (I Cor. 12:8-10). Paul also tells us that we should "strive eagerly for the spiritual gifts" (I Cor. 14:1) so that we can help build up Christ's Body, the Church. Pray for these gifts for yourself and for the whole Church. Pray for other gifts as the Holy Spirit leads you. And so we pray

- **that the Holy Spirit will produce in us, and in the Church, the gifts of the Holy Spirit, especially the gift(s) of (_____).**

The prophet Isaiah lists other gifts of the Holy Spirit—wisdom, understanding, counsel, strength (fortitude), knowledge, piety and fear of the Lord (Is. 11:2-3). Choose one or more of these gifts that you especially want the Holy Spirit to produce in you. We pray

- **that the Holy Spirit will produce in us the gifts listed by the prophet Isaiah, especially the gift(s) of (_____).**

Other specials gifts of the Holy Spirit to pray for in this decade of the rosary are:

- for the Spirit of Truth, to bring us true revelation of God and of his mysteries.
- for the Spirit of Freedom, that we might live in the true "freedom of the children of God" (Rom. 8:21; II Cor. 3:17; Gal. 5:13; John 8:31-32).
- for the Spirit of Prayer, that the Spirit will intercede for us and in us according to God's will (Rom. 8:26-28; I Cor.. 3:18).
- that the Spirit who leads the children of God would lead and guide us in all our ways (Rom. 8:14).
- that the Holy Spirit will guide and inspire the mission of the Church and her witness to Jesus (Acts 1:8; 16:6-8).
- for the Spirit of Unity, that the church and all people be united through the bond of peace in one faith, one baptism, and in the one God who is Father of all (Eph. 4:3-6).
- for the Spirit of Peace to be poured out on the whole world.
- that the Holy Spirit, the Paraclete, will comfort and console all who are suffering, especially (_____) (Eph. 14:16,25-26; 15:26; II Cor. 1:3-7).
- that the Holy Spirit will convict us, and the whole world, of sin and so bring us to true repentance (John 16:8).
- that the Holy Spirit will so transform us and unite us to Jesus that we might become living members of his Body (I Cor. 12:12-31).

As an act of faith you may conclude this decade of the rosary by praying:
We thank you, Father, for giving us the grace we have asked for through this holy mystery.

You may wish to add your own intentions below.

THE ASSUMPTION OF MARY INTO HEAVEN

Revelation 12:1; Song of Songs 2:4.

The Bible tells us that God has taken some people into heaven body and soul. "By faith Enoch was taken up so that he should not see death, and 'he was found no more because God had taken him'" (Heb. 11:5 and Gen. 5:24). The prophet Elijah also "went up to heaven in a whirlwind" (II Kings 2:11). How much more appropriate is it that God would grant this same favor to his Mother. It was right that the body of Mary—which had given Jesus his body—should "not undergo corruption" (Ps. 16:10).

Mary's assumption into heaven in many ways parallels the ascension of Jesus.

In heaven Mary joins her Son in making intercession for us. She is our heavenly advocate. She is still in the travails of childbirth until Christ is formed in us. (See Revelation 12:2 and Galatians 4:19.) Rightly then do we ask the Mother of Jesus to pray for us.[36] And so we pray

- **that Mary will be our advocate and intercede for us to obtain the graces for which we ask (especially _____).**

From heaven Mary also joins her Son in doing battle against Satan and the forces of evil. She is the bitter enemy of the dragon who does not succeed in destroying her (Rev. 12:1-6). When Jesus leads the heavenly

---

36   For a further explanation of the intercession of Mary and of the saints, see Part III, Chapter 3: "The Hail Mary," the section "Pray for us sinners...," on pages 156-157.

armies in battle, he is accompanied by the saints who are "wearing clean white linen" (Rev. 19:14). Certainly among these heavenly warriors is his Mother. And so in this decade of the rosary

- **we ask Jesus to come with Mary and all the armies of heaven, to do battle for us against the forces of evil (especially the evil of _____).**

In Mary's assumption we see the reward of her humility. In her "Magnificat" Mary refers to her "lowliness" and then speaks prophetically of her assumption when she says, "he raised the lowly to high places" (Lk. 1:52). In this mystery then

- **we ask Mary to teach us how to be humble servants of God and of our brothers and sisters, so that we too might deserve to be sharers in her assumption.** (See James 4:10.)

By raising his Mother to the glory of heaven, Jesus honored his Mother (Ex. 20:12) and fulfilled the prophecy that all ages would call Mary blessed (Lk. 1:48). And so we pray

- **that together with Jesus we will always give Mary fitting honor and love.**

Through her assumption Mary was confirmed by God in perfect holiness. In a preeminent way Mary fulfilled the prayer of St. Paul that we be "perfectly holy," and that "entirely, spirit, soul, and body" we be "preserved blameless for the coming of our Lord Jesus Christ" (I Thes. 5:23). And so we pray

- **that through Mary's assumption we may be made perfectly holy and be preserved blameless in spirit, soul, and body for the coming of our Lord Jesus Christ** (I Thes. 5:23).
- **that with Mary we may "live as children of light" and so produce "every kind of goodness and righteousness and truth"** (Eph. 5:8-9).
- **that we may learn from Mary, Elijah, and Enoch how to walk in loving communion with God** (Gen. 5:24) **and so deserve to live with God forever in heaven.**

Mary was taken up into heaven because she was not attached to this earth. Mary lived her life as a "citizen of heaven" (Phil. 3:20). Throughout her entire life Mary lived the resurrected life described by Paul: "If then you were raised with Christ, seek what is above, where Christ is seated at the right hand of God. Think of what is above, not of what is on earth. For you have died, and your life is hidden with Christ in God" (Col. 3:1-3). There was nothing in Mary that would keep her bound to this earth. And so we pray in this decade of the rosary

- **that Mary will obtain for us a detachment from an unhealthy clinging to the things of this world and a wholehearted attachment to the things of God.**

Through Mary's assumption, earth is joined to heaven and heaven is joined to earth. And so we pray

- **that through Mary's assumption into heaven the whole earth will be filled with the glory of God and all peoples will live as citizens of heaven.**
- **that through Mary's assumption, God's will may be done "on earth as it is in heaven"** (Lord's Prayer).

As an act of faith you may conclude this decade of the rosary by praying:
We thank you, Father, for giving us the grace we have asked for through this holy mystery.

You may wish to add your own intentions below.

THE CROWNING OF MARY
AS QUEEN

Revelation 12:1-6; Psalm 45:10b; II Timothy 2:12.

That Mary is Queen follows from the fact that Jesus is King. The Mother of the King must be a Queen. The author of Hebrews identifies the king of Psalm 45 as Jesus. (See Hebrews 1:8-9.) This same psalm also says, "The queen takes her place at your right hand in gold of Ophir" (Ps. 45:10). If Jesus is the King in this psalm, who is the Queen, if not his Mother?

Scripture speaks frequently of the crown that awaits us all in heaven if we remain faithful to God.[37] And Paul assures us that "if we hold out to the end, we shall also reign with him" (II Tim. 2:12). If someday we will all reign with Christ, we should not be surprised that Mary now reigns with him in heaven.

If Jesus reigns in heaven in order to fill the earth with heavenly blessings, should we not suppose that Mary assists him in this work? Scripture tells us that all Christians are "stewards of the mysteries of God" (I Cor. 4:1; I Pt. 4:10). How much more is Mary a steward and dispenser of God's mysteries. To dispense his mysteries and graces, God has given to the members of his church many roles of service, such as "apostles, prophets, evangelists, pastors and teachers" (Eph. 5:11). All these roles of service are limited in their scope. The role of Mother and Queen, however, is an *unlimited* and *universal* role, reaching to every member of the church of all time.

---

37   See II Timothy 4:8, James 1:12, I Peter 5:4, Revelation 2:10, 3:11 and 4:4.

To be a steward, or dispenser of God's graces, is to be a "mediator." Jesus alone is the Mediator as the SOURCE of all graces. But all Christians in their assigned roles of service are *stewards* or *distributors* of these graces. Mary, in her role as Queen and as Mother of all Christians, has a universal role as *distributor, steward,* or *mediator* of God's graces. We honor the role that God has given Mary by asking her to exercise her motherly and queenly role in our lives. And so we pray

- in thanksgiving to God for giving us such a loving and solicitous Mother and Queen.
- for those who need to know the love and tender care of a mother (especially _____), that they may experience the motherly love and care of Mary.
- that Mary would obtain from her Son the "New Wine" of the Holy Spirit and so bring about a new Pentecost for the Church and for the world.
- that Mary would obtain from her Son the special grace for which we now ask (_____).
- that Mary, in her role as Mother, would obtain for _____ the grace to be born again as a child of God. (See John 3:3-8.)
- that as Mary takes her place at the right hand of the King "in gold of Ophir" (Ps. 45:10), she will obtain for us the grace to live even now as citizens of the golden city (Rev. 21:18).

God's word tells us that "the Lord withholds no good thing from those who walk without reproach" (Ps. 84:12). How then could the Lord withhold any good thing from his Mother who always walked without reproach before him? And so

- we pray with confidence that God will not withhold the good things we ask for through the intercession of Mary (especially the following graces _____).

Mary exercises her queenly role in the same way that Jesus exercises his kingly role, namely by serving others. And so we ask

- that Mary, in her role as Queen, would obtain for all those in authority the grace to exercise their authority with gentleness, with humility, and with care for the poor and the weak.

As an act of faith you may conclude this decade of the rosary by praying:
We thank you, Father, for giving us the grace we have asked for through this holy mystery.

You may wish to add your own intentions below.

PART III

MAKING OUR PRAYER
MORE EFFECTIVE

CHAPTER 11

RECEIVING
WHAT IS OURS

"Who will give you what is yours?"

Luke 16:12

How can we speak of receiving what is already ours? If it is ours, don't we already possess it? Yes and no. A person may have inherited his parents' estate, but he must go through the required legal process in order to actually take possession of it. A person may have won the lottery, but he must go and claim it by submitting the winning numbers. Or we may have a great deal of money locked away in a safe, but if we have forgotten the combination, we won't be able to open it and use what is ours.

In the same way, we may have many spiritual treasures stored up for us in God's "storehouses," treasures that are ours by right, but if we are to make them truly our own, we must first learn what these treasures are, claim them, and then use them for God's glory. Otherwise, many of our gifts will simply remain "on hold" for us.

St. Paul talked about this problem when he said, "I mean that as long as the heir is not of age, he is no different from a slave, although he is the owner of everything" (Gal. 4:1). Paul recognized that even though we are all heirs of God's promises, we may not yet have "come of age." We may still be living in ignorance of what is ours and of how to lay claim to it. Or we may be living in a way that prevents us from receiving what is ours. Recall how the father, in the parable of the Prodigal Son, assured his older son, "My son...everything I have is yours" (Lk. 15:31). And yet that son was not disposed in his heart to receive it.

And so as we begin to pray the rosary for intercession and spiritual victory, and seek to claim our inheritance, it is important to learn how to do this most effectively. Let us look now at those dispositions of mind and heart that make us most receptive to receive God's gifts. In the next chapter we will look at ways to make our prayer more effective.

The Example of Mary

God has given us Mary to teach us how to receive. She received the Gift which contains all other gifts—her divine Son. She is rightly called "Full of Grace" because she received ALL of God's gifts and graces. She will teach us how to do it as well.

Surrender to God's Will. "Behold, I am the handmaid of the Lord. May it be done to me according to your word" (Lk. 1:38). If we are to receive God's gifts we must be surrendered to God's will. Our constant attitude, like Mary's, must be to be God's servants—ready to do God's will at all times and to use our gifts only for God's glory and not our own.

Be Humble of Heart. "He has looked upon his handmaid's lowliness" (Lk. 1:48). We receive God's gifts when we know, like Mary, that of ourselves we are nothing. Jesus told us that we must become "poor in spirit" if we are to inherit the kingdom of heaven (Mt. 5:3).

Be Hungry for God. "The hungry he has filled with good things" (Lk. 1:53). Like Mary we hunger for the things of God. We "think of what is above, not of what is on earth" (Col. 3:1). We empty ourselves of self-will and of self-importance.

Make Jesus your Treasure. Mary's treasure was always and only Jesus. If we make Jesus our treasure, all good things will be ours as well. (See also Psalm 37:4.)

Other Essential Dispositions[38]

Forgive those who have hurt you. If we forgive those who have hurt us, we will be open to receive God's gift of forgiveness. If we show mercy to others, we will receive God's mercy. (See Sirach 28:3-4; Matthew 5:7; Mark 11:25; and Luke. 6:36.)

Be reconciled. Paul says, "If possible, on your part, live at peace with all" (Rom. 12:18). If we refuse to be reconciled with others, then Jesus tells us not to offer our gifts at the altar. "Go first," he says, "and be reconciled with your brother" (Mt. 5:24). We might also conclude that if we are not to offer our gifts at the altar, we will also not receive God's gifts from the altar.

Be generous in giving God's Gifts to others. "Give and gifts will be given to you; a good measure, packed together, shaken down, and overflowing, will be poured into your lap" (Lk. 6:38). (See also I Peter 4:10.)

Love all People. We must have expanded hearts like the heart of Jesus to love everyone in the world. Jesus loves everyone, and he died to save everyone without exception. The Fatima prayer that is often said at the conclusion of each decade of the rosary helps us with this. We pray, "Lead all souls to heaven, especially those in most need of your mercy." Indeed we are to love all of God's creation. God is "compassionate to every creature" (Ps. 145:9). If we exclude anyone from our love, we narrow our hearts and make them less able to receive God's gifts. It is like someone who buys a beautiful new couch for his home, only to

---

38   In listing these other dispositions separately we do not imply that these were not qualities of Mary, but only that they are listed in scriptures that do not directly speak of Mary. These qualities Mary also exemplified to an extraordinary degree.

142

discover when he brings it home that the doors of his house are too narrow for the couch to enter.

Treat others with Respect and Honor. St. Peter reminds husbands that they should show honor to their wives so that their "prayers may not be hindered" (I Pt. 3:7). We might also think of the honor we show to the elderly, to the sick, to the poor, and to children. When we help those in need, we are helping Jesus himself. "Whatever you did for one of these least brothers of mine, you did for me" (Mt. 25:40). Jesus in turn will be generous to us.

Seek Purity of Heart. As we seek through prayer to receive more of God's gifts, we need to pray for purity of heart. "A clean heart create for me, God" (Ps. 51:12). God wants to put his gifts in a clean container. Mary's heart was a pure vessel ready to receive God's gifts. Ask her to obtain this same purity of heart for you.

Put on Christ and abide in him. "If you remain in me and my words remain in you, ask for whatever you want and it will be done for you" (John 15:7). Remaining in Jesus is like living in the palace of the King with a key to every room. Or better yet, it is like living in heaven with access to the Holy of Holies. St. Paul uses the metaphor of clothing when he writes, "Put on the Lord Jesus Christ and make no provision for the desires of the flesh" (Rom. 13:14). Putting on Christ and abiding in him will mean dying to oneself. "Those who belong to Christ Jesus have crucified their flesh with its passions and desires" (Gal. 5:24).[39] Like attracts like. The likeness of Christ in you will attract even more of God's gifts.

Live by the Spirit. The Holy Spirit will teach you what is pleasing to God (Col. 1:10). Continual surrender to the Holy Spirit will give the Spirit freedom to work in you and to fill you with his gifts. Frequently

---

39   Read Paul's description of our new life in Christ in Ephesians 4:17-5:5.

ask the Holy Spirit to create in you the nature and likeness of Jesus and to remove from you all that is contrary to Jesus.[40]

Be faithful in small things.
Be faithful to the call that God has given you—even in small things. Jesus puts great importance on this. He relates being faithful to our "worldly" duties to our ability to be entrusted with spiritual gifts. "If, therefore, you are not trustworthy with dishonest wealth, who will trust you with true wealth? If you are not trustworthy with what belongs to another, who will give you what is yours?" (Lk. 16:11-12). The spiritual gifts of heaven are ours by right. Yet God cannot entrust them to us if we are unfaithful in the little things he has given us to do.

Empty yourself together with Jesus. Jesus "emptied himself, taking the form of a slave" (Phil. 2:7). "Because of this, God greatly exalted him and bestowed on him the name that is above every name" (Phil. 2:9). Jesus emptied himself of all that was not the Father's will. Because of this he was able to receive his full inheritance and to bestow it on us. In the same way, if we are to receive our full inheritance, we too must empty ourselves of all self-will and inordinate attachment to creatures. As long as we are full of self and selfish desires, we will not have room to receive all that God wants to give us. Even if you are not living a life of sin, you may still be clinging to the things of this world in a way that keeps you from surrendering fully to God. If your house is full of your own things, there will be little room for the things of God.

---

40   To deepen this work of the Holy Spirit in you, read and pray the following scriptures: Galatians 5:13-26; Romans 8:2-13; I John 2:15-16.

CHAPTER 12

EFFECTIVE PRAYER

*"The prayer of the lowly pierces the clouds;
it does not rest till it reaches its goal,
nor will it withdraw till the Most High responds."*

Sirach 35:17–18

In the last chapter we looked at ways to open ourselves to receive more of God's gifts and blessings—in fact to receive our full inheritance. In this chapter we will look at various ways that our prayer can become more effective. The rosary in itself is "designed" to be an effective prayer, but it can become more effective when we learn how to pray it better. I might possess a tool that can create beautiful objects out of wood or metal, but unless I learn how to use it, the tool will remain unproductive. Or I might have a set of very fine brushes for painting and the widest variety of colors, but if I don't know how to use the brushes and the colors, there will be no work of art.

Here are some suggestions to make your prayer more effective. You may not consciously begin each rosary with each of these suggestions in mind, but it would be good to review them from time to time.

Pray with Jesus

Using the analogy of the paintbrush, put your hand with your paintbrush in the hand of Jesus and let him guide it. He will make just the right strokes and use just the right colors to create a beautiful work of art. The author of Hebrews says that Jesus lives forever to make intercession for us (Heb. 7:25). He is always praying for us in the presence of his Father. He wants to take your prayer and join it to his own perfect prayer. Jesus' prayer is always heard, as Jesus himself said, "Father…I know that you always hear me" (John 11:41-42). Our prayer (whether the rosary or other prayers), joined with the prayer of Jesus, will always be heard.

Pray and Ask in the Name of Jesus

Praying and asking "in the name of Jesus" is really another way of joining our prayer to Jesus' heavenly intercession. Again, we rely on Jesus to make our prayer his own prayer. "Until now you have not asked anything in my name; ask and you will receive, so that your joy may be complete" (John 16:26). (See also John 14:14 and 15:16.)

Invite the Holy Spirit to Pray in You

"We do not know how to pray as we ought," Paul says. But he also adds that the Spirit "comes to the aid of our weakness" and "intercedes with inexpressible groanings" (Rom. 8:26). The prayer of the Holy Spirit is likewise always heard, as Paul goes on to say, "And the one who searches hearts knows what is the intention of the Spirit, because it intercedes for the holy ones according to God's will" (Rom. 8:27). Again, with each rosary, ask the Holy Spirit to pray in you.

Unite your Prayer to the Heavenly Intercession of Mary, the Angels, and the Saints

We recall in the gospels how Mary interceded with Jesus at the wedding feast at Cana and obtained the best wine for the wedding. After Jesus ascended to heaven she interceded with Jesus again and she, and the first disciples, obtained the New Wine of the Holy Spirit at Pentecost. (See Acts 1:14.) Mary continues to intercede for us, as do the other saints and the angels in heaven.[41] And so as we pray the rosary we entrust our prayers to Mary, to her loving heart, and we join our prayers to the prayers of all the blessed in heaven.

Pray with Faith

As we visit the heavenly storehouses of the mysteries of Christ and ask for the gifts that are stored up for us there, we ask for them in faith. This sounds very simple, but we know from experience that faith does not come easily. We often struggle like the father of the demonized child who said to Jesus, "I do believe, help my unbelief!" (Mk. 9:24). And yet, if we have followed the steps suggested above, we have every confidence that our prayer is heard. We have united our prayer to the prayer of Jesus as he makes intercession for us. God will not refuse the prayer of his Son. We have surrendered our prayer to the Holy Spirit who "intercedes for the holy ones according to God's will" (Rom. 8:26). And we have put our prayer in the hands and heart of Mary and joined it with the intercession of the blessed in heaven. How could we doubt that our prayer will be answered?[42]

---

41   Recall how the 24 elders offer our prayers to God (Rev. 5:8) and how the martyrs in heaven intercede for justice to be done on the earth. See Revelation 6:9-10. The angels too offer our prayers to God. See Revelation 8:3-4. Recall also the heavenly intercession of Jeremiah as described in II Maccabees 15:13-16.

42   To help build your faith, read and pray the following scriptures: Matthew 18:19; Mark 11:22-24; Luke 11:9-13; John 14:13-14; 15:7,16; 16:24; I John 5:14-15.

As a way of confessing your faith, I have suggested that at the conclusion of each decade of the rosary, you express your belief that God has answered your prayer by praying, "We thank you, Father, for giving us the grace we have asked for through this holy mystery."

Pray with Humility

"The prayer of the lowly pierces the clouds; it does not rest till it reaches its goal, nor will it withdraw till the Most High responds" (Sirach 35:17-18). Mary gives us an example of humility. She recognized that God had "looked upon his handmaid's lowliness" (Lk. 1:48). Her lowliness, as it were, caught the eye of God, and God came down to lift her up. And Mary adds that the same is true for us. God always lifts up the lowly (Lk. 1:52; I Pt. 5:6). Confess your own nothingness to God and confess the "allness" of Jesus, and your prayer will be heard. (See also Esther, Chapter C, verses 14, 25, and 29.)

Pray with Perseverance

God sometimes keeps us waiting before he answers our prayers. We would like to know why God does this. In fact God doesn't tell us why, but he does tell us that persistence gets results!

Recall the parable of the person who went to his friend at midnight and asked for three loaves of bread. Even though his friend didn't want to get up in the middle of the night, Jesus tells us that "he will get up to give him whatever he needs because of his persistence" (Lk. 11:8). The parable of the persistent widow is similar. She kept coming to the judge day after day demanding, "Render a just decision for me against my adversary" (Lk. 18:3). Although for a long time the judge resisted, he finally gave in "because this widow keeps bothering me" (Lk. 18:5). Jesus says of this, "Will not God then secure the rights of his chosen ones who call out to him day and night? Will he be slow to answer them? I tell you, he will see to it that justice is done for them speedily" (Lk. 18:7-8).

Pray with Gratitude

Paul says that even our prayers of petition should be made "with thanksgiving" (Phil. 4:6). We thank God not only for the gifts we have already received, but also for the gifts that we will receive from His hands. Thanksgiving opens for us the storehouses of heaven.

Be Specific

God wants us to ask Him for what we need. When the blind man, Bartimaeus, asked Jesus to have pity on him, Jesus asked him, "What do you want me to do for you?" (Mk. 10:51; also Mt. 20:32 and Lk. 18:41) Jesus certainly knew what the blind man needed, but he wanted the man himself to express his need. Like the child who asked his father for a loaf of bread or for a fish (Mt. 7:9-10) and so received them from his father, so we too ask our heavenly Father for specific gifts. In this way, when we receive them, we will know that these blessings come from the hands of our Father and we will give him the thanks that he deserves. I have also suggested that you keep a prayer journal, recording both the intentions prayed for and God's answer to these prayers.[43]

The Gift and the Challenge of Repetitive Prayer

In his Apostolic Letter on the rosary, Pope John Paul II recalled the teaching of Pope Paul VI on the rosary as a contemplative prayer. Pope Paul VI tells us:

> "Without contemplation, the Rosary is a body without a soul, and its recitation runs the risk of becoming a mechanical repetition of formulas, in violation of the admonition of Christ: 'In praying do not heap up empty phrases as the Gentiles do; for they think they

---

43   See Appendix I for a beginning of this journal.

> will be heard for their many words' (Mt. 6:7). By its
> nature the recitation of the Rosary calls for a quiet
> rhythm and a lingering pace, helping the individual
> to meditate on the mysteries of the Lord's life as seen
> through the eyes of her who was closest to the Lord.
> In this way the unfathomable riches of these mysteries
> are disclosed."[44]

It is important to be aware that it is not the repetition of prayers as such that Jesus is condemning in the gospel, but rather the mentality that supposes that the more prayers we say, the greater will be the results. God is not interested in how **many** prayers we say, but on how **sincere** and heartfelt our prayer is.

The repetition of prayers and prayer phrases is actually very biblical. Recall the repetition in Psalm 136 of the refrain, "God's love endures forever." It is repeated 26 times! In Psalm 46 we hear the beautiful refrain, "The Lord of hosts is with us; our stronghold is the God of Jacob" (Ps. 46:4,8,12). And in Psalm 67 we find the refrain, "May the peoples praise you, God; may all the peoples praise you!" (Ps. 67:4,6). The angels also continue to cry out, "Holy, holy, holy" before the throne of God (Is. 6:3).

Repetition can serve to deepen in us the reality of the prayer we are repeating. Christian tradition also offers us the "Jesus Prayer" in which the prayer "Lord Jesus Christ, Son of God, have mercy on me, a sinner" is repeated over and over. Abbot David Geraets, OSB, once said, "You know you're beginning to pray when you can say the name of Jesus a thousand times without repeating yourself."

The repeated prayers of the rosary likewise can produce wonderful effects in us. But we can't rush through them. We pray them rather, as

---

44   Apostolic Letter of Pope John Paul II *Rosarium Virginis Mariae*, 12.

Pope Paul VI, says, with a "quiet rhythm and a lingering pace." Better a decade of the rosary prayed with heartfelt love and devotion than ten rosaries said mechanically.

You might want to list here other qualities of prayer that you have found to be important. What has the Holy Spirit taught you about prayer?

CHAPTER 13

THE HAIL MARY

"Behold, from now on will all ages call me blessed."
Luke 1:48

The most repeated prayer of the rosary is the "Hail Mary." After praying the "Hail Mary" three times before we begin the five decades, we then pray it ten times for each mystery. And so it is important to understand this prayer and the role that it plays in the rosary.

Many Christians who are not familiar with Catholic prayer traditions find the "Hail Mary" to be an awkward and puzzling kind of prayer. It can even appear to be an unbiblical way to pray. Let us examine each section of this prayer separately to discover its deeper nature and meaning.

Hail Mary, full of grace, the Lord is with you. *(Luke 1:28)*

Immediately we notice, as we begin this prayer, that it is addressed to Mary, whereas most prayers are directed immediately to God—Father, Son, or Holy Spirit. Actually the prayer begins with **God's** address to Mary through the angel Gabriel.

Many prayers in the bible contain, and even begin with, God's word addressed to us. This might well be expected if indeed prayer is a dialogue between God and ourselves. Here are a few examples. "Listen, my people, I will speak; Israel, I will testify against you; God, your God, am I" (Ps. 50:7). "In distress you called and I rescued you; unseen, I spoke to you in thunder" (Ps. 81:8).

Sometimes in prayer we repeat what God says to another. For example God says to the Messiah: "You are my son; today I am your father" (Ps. 2:7). God also says to the Messiah: "Take your throne at my right hand...Rule over your enemies...Like Melchizedek you are a priest forever" (Ps. 110:1,2,4).

When we pray these prayers we are repeating the words that God addresses to his Messiah and to us. We do the same when we pray the "Hail Mary." We repeat the words that God addressed to Mary. We are addressing Mary together with God.

Blessed are you among women

Again, in this part of the Hail Mary, we are repeating the words that God addressed to Mary—this time through Mary's relative, Elizabeth. By saying these words we are also being obedient to God by fulfilling the prophecy that he gave through Mary herself, "Behold, from now on will all ages call me blessed" (Lk. 1:48). Christians of every age are invited to fulfill this prophecy by calling Mary "blessed." Elizabeth was the first. We follow in her footsteps.

Blessed is the fruit of your womb, Jesus

We also bless Jesus as the Son of God made flesh in the womb of Mary. Blessing God is certainly a major part of biblical prayer.[45]

---

45   See for example Psalm 34:1: "I will bless the Lord at all times." Also Psalm 134:1: "Come, bless the Lord." And Psalm 144:1: "Blessed be the Lord, my rock."

Holy Mary, Mother of God

In the first half of the "Hail Mary" we heard God, our Father, addressing Mary through the angel Gabriel and through Elizabeth. In the second half of the prayer, we imitate God by doing the same. It is as if God were saying, "I have just shown you how to address Mary. Now I invite you to address Mary in your own words. Tell her what is on your mind and heart."[46]

We begin by addressing Mary with two titles, "Holy" and "Mother of God."

The title "holy" is certainly appropriate for Mary. We need only think of what the angel Gabriel said to her, "The holy Spirit will come upon you, and the power of the Most High will overshadow you" (Lk. 1:35). We recall also that Paul does not hesitate to call all Christians holy, as he does for example in his letter to the Philippians—"to all the holy ones in Christ Jesus who are in Philippi" (Phil. 1:1).

We also address Mary as "Mother of God." We should not imagine that it was "only the Church" who in later centuries applied this title to Mary. Elizabeth in fact was the first, when she said to Mary, "And how does this happen to me, that the mother of my Lord should come to me?" (Lk. 1:43). The apostle Thomas likewise professed his faith in Jesus

---

46   Addressing those who are in heaven rests on the biblical precedent of Jesus himself when he conversed with Moses and Elijah on the mount of Transfiguration. See Luke 9:30-31. Occasionally God allows an even more immediate contact with the saints as we read in Matthew 27:52-53, "The bodies of many saints who had fallen asleep were raised. And coming forth from their tombs after his resurrection, they entered the holy city and appeared to many." Any such appearances must be very carefully discerned to avoid the deception of Satan who can appear as "an angel of light" (II Cor. 11:14). However, this should not obscure the reality of the Communion of Saints in which we have fellowship not only with the angels and with the saints on earth, but also with "the spirits of the just made perfect" (Heb. 12:23), that is, with the saints in heaven.

as "My Lord and my God!" (John 20:28) Putting these two scriptures together, we can call Mary, "Mother of my Lord and my God." Or we can shorten it to say simply "Mother of God."

Pray for us sinners now and at the hour of our death

We now ask Mary to pray for us. We ask her to join her Son, Jesus, who in heaven "lives forever to make intercession" for us. (Hebrews 7:25) If the saints in heaven in fact "follow the Lamb wherever he goes" (Rev. 14:4), we can also be sure that in heaven they also do whatever the Lamb does, namely make intercession for us.[47]

Mary is our fellow intercessor, as we too are called to make intercession "for all the holy ones" (Eph. 6:18).

We catch a little glimpse of the effectiveness of Mary's intercession when she obtains from her Son his first miracle of changing water into wine at the wedding at Cana. (See John 2:1-11.) Mary continued her intercession for the early Church, joining with other disciples of Jesus to pray for the coming of the Holy Spirit at Pentecost. See the Acts of the Apostles 1:13-14.

Rightly then do we ask Mary to pray for us.

We ask Mary to pray for us NOW! Our needs are immediate. We need help from heaven NOW. We ask Mary to approach the throne of grace with us "to receive mercy and to find grace for timely help" (Heb. 4:16).

---

47   In Revelation 6:10 we see the saints in heaven interceding and asking God to intervene on the earth. Recall also the vision given to Judas Maccabeus of the prophet Jeremiah. In this vision Judas was told, "This is God's prophet Jeremiah, who loves his brethren and fervently prays for his people and their holy city" (II Macc. 15:14). That the saints in heaven can continue to help us is also illustrated by the story recounted in II Kings 13:20-21. Here a man is raised from the dead by being thrown into the grave of the prophet Elisha. And so it was said of Elisha: "In life he performed wonders and after death marvelous deeds" (Sirach 48:14).

If we are praying the mysteries of the rosary, our request for graces NOW could be to receive those particular graces contained in the mystery we are now praying—as we have suggested earlier in this book.

We also ask Mary to pray for us "at the hour of our death." The moment of death is an especially crucial time for us. The forces of hell do all in their power to take our souls away from God for all eternity. They try especially to make us doubt that we can be saved, to doubt that God has forgiven our sins, and so to bring us to despair. They also try to harden our hearts toward God, to make us persist in our sins. At this time especially we need the prayers of the sinless Mother of God. She brings with her the grace and mercy of her Son. She who stood by the cross of Jesus brings with her the atoning and saving blood of her Son and with it her Son's gift of "eternal redemption" (Heb. 9:12).

More effective prayer

Does the "Hail Mary" make our prayer more effective? By all means! It joins our prayers to the prayers of Mary—and in fact to the prayers of all the angels and saints in heaven—and with them to the prayers of Jesus. If the prayers of "two or more" joining their voices on earth are effective, how much more effective will they be when they are joined with the prayers of Mary and all the blessed in heaven?

APPENDIX I

TEMPLATE FOR A PRAYER JOURNAL

Intention prayed for and dates.

God's answered prayer and date.

Intention prayed for and dates.

God's answered prayer and date.

Intention prayed for and dates.

God's answered prayer and date.

Intention prayed for and dates.

God's answered prayer and date.

Intention prayed for and dates.

God's answered prayer and date.

Intention prayed for and dates.

God's answered prayer and date.

Intention prayed for and dates.

God's answered prayer and date.

APPENDIX II

THE PRAYERS OF THE ROSARY

The Sign of the Cross *(At the beginning—holding the crucifix)*
In the name of the Father, and of the Son, and of the Holy Spirit. Amen.

The Apostles Creed *(Following the Sign of the Cross)*
I believe in God, the Father almighty, creator of heaven and earth. And in Jesus Christ, his only Son, our Lord, who was conceived by the Holy Spirit, born of the Virgin Mary, suffered under Pontius Pilate; was crucified, died, and was buried. He descended into hell. The third day he rose again from the dead. He ascended into heaven and sits at the right hand of God, the Father almighty. From thence he shall come to judge the living and the dead. I believe in the Holy Spirit, the holy Catholic Church, the communion of saints, the forgiveness of sins, the resurrection of the body, and life everlasting. Amen.

The following text of the Apostles Creed, approved by the US Conference of Catholic Bishops, is sometimes used instead of the more traditional version given above:
I believe in God, the Father almighty, creator of heaven and earth. I believe in Jesus Christ, his only Son, our Lord. He was conveyed by the power of the Holy Spirit and born of the Virgin Mary. He suffered under Pontius Pilate, was crucified, died, and was buried. He descended to the dead. On the third day he rose again. He ascended into heaven, and is seated at the right hand of the Father. He will come again to judge the living and the dead. I believe in the Holy Spirit, the holy catholic Church, the communion of saints, the forgiveness of sins, the resurrection of the body, and the life everlasting. Amen

The Our Father *(At the first bead and at the beginning of each decade)*
Our Father, who art in heaven, hallowed be thy name; thy kingdom come; thy will be done on earth as it is in heaven. Give us this day our daily bread; and forgive us our trespasses as we forgive those who trespass against us; and lead us not into temptation, but deliver us from evil. Amen.

The Hail Mary *(With the three beads after the first Our Father and with the 10 beads that follow the Our Father of each decade)*
Hail Mary, full of grace, the Lord is with thee. Blessed art thou among women and blessed is the fruit of thy womb, Jesus. Holy Mary, Mother of God, pray for us sinners now and at the hour of our death. Amen.

The "Glory be" (Doxology) *(After each decade)*
Glory be to the Father, and to the Son, and to the Holy Spirit. As it was in the beginning, is now, and ever shall be, world without end. Amen.

The Fatima Prayer *(After each decade)*
O my Jesus, forgive us our sins. Save us from the fires of hell. Lead all souls to heaven, especially those in most need of thy mercy. Amen.

Prayer of Thanksgiving *(After each decade as suggested in this book)*
We thank you, Father, for giving us the grace we have asked for through this holy mystery.

The Hail Holy Queen *(After the last decade)*
Hail holy Queen, mother of mercy; our life, our sweetness, and our hope. To thee do we cry, poor banished children of Eve. To thee do we send up our sighs, mourning and weeping in this valley of tears. Turn then, most gracious advocate, thine eyes of mercy toward us. And after this, our exile, show unto us the blessed fruit of thy womb, Jesus. O clement, O loving, O sweet Virgin Mary. Pray for us, O holy Mother of God, that we may be made worthy of the promises of Christ.

Traditional Concluding Prayer *(After the Hail Holy Queen)*
O God, whose only begotten Son, by his life, death, and resurrection has purchased for us the rewards of eternal life, grant we beseech Thee that by meditating on these mysteries of the most holy rosary of the Blessed Virgin Mary, we may imitate what they contain and obtain what they promise through the same Christ our Lord. Amen.

Prayer to St. Michael *(This prayer is also sometimes said after the Rosary)*
St. Michael, the archangel, defend us in battle. Be our protection against
the wickedness and snares of the devil. May God rebuke him, we humbly
pray, and do thou, O Prince of the Heavenly Host, by the power of God,
cast into hell Satan and all the evil spirits who prowl about the world
seeking the ruin of souls. Amen.

APPENDIX III

MY BEADS[48]

Sweet, blessed beads! I would not part
    With one of you for richest gem
    That gleams in kingly diadem;
Ye know the history of my heart.

For I have told you every grief
    In all the days of twenty years,
    And I have moistened you with tears,
And in your decades found relief.

Ah! time has fled, and friends have failed
    And joys have died; but in my needs
    Ye were my friends, my blessed beads!
And ye consoled me when I wailed.

For many and many a time, in grief,
    My weary fingers wandered round
    Thy circled chain, and always found
In some Hail Mary sweet relief.

How many a story you might tell
    Of inner life, to all unknown;
    I trusted you and you alone,
But ah! ye keep my secrets well.

---

48   This poem was written by Fr. Abram Ryan, known during the American Civil War as "The Poet Priest of the South." Fr. Abram J. Ryan, *Poems: Patriotic, Religious, Miscellaneous*, (P. J. Kenedy& Sons, 1896), 151.

Ye are the only chain I wear—
      A sign that I am but the slave,
      In life, in death, beyond the grave,
Of Jesus and His Mother fair.

CPSIA information can be obtained at www.ICGtesting.com
234920LV00002B/2/P